T0147157

# The God of Restoration

ANITA M. PAYTON

WESTBOW
PRESS®
A DIVISION OF THOMAS NELSON
& ZONDERVAN

WestBow Press books may be ordered through booksellers or by contacting:

WestBow Press
A Division of Thomas Nelson & Zondervan
1663 Liberty Drive
Bloomington, IN 47403
www.westbowpress.com
844-714-3454

Because of the dynamic nature of the Internet, any web addresses or links contained in this book may have changed since publication and may no longer be valid. The views expressed in this work are solely those of the author and do not necessarily reflect the views of the publisher, and the publisher hereby disclaims any responsibility for them.

Any people depicted in stock imagery provided by Getty Images are models, and such images are being used for illustrative purposes only. Certain stock imagery © Getty Images.

Unless otherwise indicated, all Scripture taken from the King James Version of the Bible.

Scripture quotations marked MSG are taken from THE MESSAGE, copyright © 1993, 2002, 2018 by Eugene H. Peterson. Used by permission of NavPress. All rights reserved. Represented by Tyndale House Publishers, a Division of Tyndale House Ministries.

Scripture quotations marked (NLT) are taken from the Holy Bible, New Living Translation, copyright ©1996, 2004, 2015 by Tyndale House Foundation. Used by permission of Tyndale House Publishers, a Division of Tyndale House Ministries, Carol Stream, Illinois 60188. All rights reserved.

ISBN: 978-1-6642-8007-6 (sc)
ISBN: 978-1-6642-8006-9 (hc)
ISBN: 978-1-6642-8008-3 (e)

Library of Congress Control Number: 2022918577

Print information available on the last page.

WestBow Press rev. date: 1/9/2023

# Contents

# Preface

One morning, some thirty years ago, I woke up and told my husband that I had dreamed I had written a book.

He casually asked, "What was it about?"

I replied, "I don't know."

That response got his attention. He proceeded to say how strange that dream must have been. It did not make much sense to him. Well, it did not make sense to me, either. All I knew was that the book's title was *The God of Restoration*. Even though I knew I was the author, I had no idea what I had actually written. The next person I told was my spiritual mother, Doretha. I was excited when she shared that she had a similar dream of writing a book. She started writing the manuscript; sadly, she passed away before it could be published.

What exactly was God going to restore? My marriage, my relationship with my biological father, my mind, and my health. Many years passed as I waited for the final chapters to unfold. At the time I had the dream of writing a book, none of these things had happened and I didn't see them coming.

Everyone has been waiting on this book for years. Well, the time has come. During a year of uncertainty for our nation and world, during a time of pandemic and quarantine, when many counted 2020 a waste and a loss, I knew it was time for my dream to be fulfilled. God makes rivers in the desert place, and because of Him, this book springs forth from tough trials and chaos. At last, the world can be inspired by my story. The following pages will give you an up close and personal peek into my life—the good, the bad, and the ugly—all the while sharing the opportunity for you to see how Jesus Christ is able to restore that which seems hopeless and beyond repair.

It has been an overwhelming assignment to start writing and actually finish. Some years ago, when I began, I had many starts and stops because of the tears that clouded my eyes as I attempted to transfer my story to paper for all the world to see. With the help of the Lord, I made up my mind to shut myself away from everything and everybody, in order to allow God to use me as His vessel by sharing my life's story to help encourage and inspire the young and the old to hold on to hope. I fought the tears and the fear in order to fulfill my purpose.

As I wrote, I looked back over my life, and I've realized that the temporal and the eternal clash; what seemed to be my beginning was the end, and what seemed to be my end was the beginning. You see, my beginning started in the mind of God before time began; therefore, my life started, it was interrupted, went off track and back on again; I was then led back to a place in time when I thought I had reached the end—only to find that, in fact, I had come back to the beginning. Whew, confusing? Yes, I must agree. However, it is my hope that, as I share my journey, you will see in your own life the times that you, too, in part, if not fully, have come full circle.

> When I consider the heavens the work of thy finger, the moon, and the stars, which Thou hast ordained; What is man that Thou art mindful of him and the son of man, that Thou visitest him? For Thou has made him a little lower than the angels and has crowned him with glory and honour. Thou madest him to have dominion over the works of Thy hands; Thou has put all things under his feet. (Psalm 8:3–6)

I've learned that I am the crown of God's creation and He's thinking about me. He's concerned about me and all that concerns me. I didn't know or believe that until I became an adult and had time to deepen my spiritual relationship with the Lord. My life's tests and trails didn't come to destroy me or make me bitter, but to make me stronger and better than before. There are always lessons to be learned. Whether God sends or permits the trouble, it's all a part of His divine plan and purpose. The mess in my life has become my MESSage of hope to those who don't believe, feel like giving up, or worry that they weren't meant to be here.

It was much later in life, when I found this life-changing passage in the Holy Bible, that I realized that my journey (the good, bad, and ugly) was leading me to an expected, hopeful, and purposeful end.

> For I know the thoughts that I think toward you, saith the LORD, thoughts of peace, and not of evil, to give you an expected end. (Jeremiah 29:11)

Perhaps you've aspired, as I have, to be like your role model or mentor because he or she seems to be smart, successful, and have it all together. Everything works in that person's favor, and he or she has plenty of money, the dream house, the nice car, the loving marriage, and the perfect children. But one day, you'll likely be surprised to find out that he or she has also been through tough trials and misfortune. Over the years, I've learned that what appears to be green grass on the other side of the fence was once a junkyard of hard, dry dirt mixed with bricks and other debris. It had to be sifted, fertilized, and cultivated. Many people hide behind nice clothes and beautiful makeup and know how to look "the part," while keeping their true stories hidden. Sadly, some aren't so eager to share the truth of their lives because they fear rejection and the judgement of others.

As I write this book, I resolve to be brave. I invite you to walk with me through my fair weather, my storms, my ups, downs, starts, and stops. It's my story, unedited, up close, and personal, and I'm sticking to it.

By God's grace, I present to the nations *The God of Restoration.* It is my prayer that it will inspire you, give you hope, resurrect your dreams, and cause you to love unconditionally! I give all glory to my Lord and Savior Jesus Christ for without Him, I would have lost my mind, my life, and the opportunity to share His amazing grace and power to restore. He is *the God of restoration*!

> Better is the end of a thing than the beginning thereof.
> (Ecclesiastes 7:8a)

# Acknowledgment

To God be all the glory for the things He has done! Thank you to my husband for his years of patience as I talked through the content, and his encouragement as I actually began to write. I'm grateful for my children, family, and friends who encouraged me along this journey. To my niece Dionne and her sister Leah for helping me edit. You both are amazing.

# Dedication

To Mom

Myrtle Virginia Peters Crisp Welch
10/09/1925—11/11/2019


To Dad

George Washington Hammond, Jr.
4/20/1927—1/4/2002

# Mom

My dear mother, Myrtle Virginia Peters Crisp Welch, was the great-great-granddaughter of slaves from the Beavercreek Plantation in Martinsville, Virginia. She went to heaven on Monday, November 11, 2019. She birthed six children. We were so spread out that it seemed like there were two families instead of one. My three older siblings—Joyce, Carol (who is deceased), and Robert (who we call Bobby)—are old enough to be my parents. They had married and started families of their own by the time I was born. They have children within one to three years of my age. Their children and I grew up like siblings.

The last three of my mother's children include Charles, who is six years older than me, and Lenore, who is four years younger than me. I was on the tail end, smack dab in the middle. Even with that lineup, we seemed to grow up as only children, each so different and in our own little worlds. We lived in the same house, but I don't recall doing very many things together as a family or as siblings. My brother Charles absolutely loved music and everything about it. He learned to play the violin and guitar at an early age and was always making melodies, singing, and playing his guitar in his bedroom. Every Christmas, he could count on getting a new guitar or something related to music. As a baby, my younger sister was like my real-live baby doll, and that's how I treated her. I'd struggle to pick her up on my hip and carry her everywhere I went. That was a lot of fun, until she grew up and wanted to do her own thing. She often reminded me that I wasn't her boss and couldn't tell her what to do.

Unfortunately, after a few separations, Mom and Deddy divorced when I was four years old. He later moved south and remarried. I vaguely recall him living in the house with us. I don't remember when he left or understand why. One day, I woke up, and he was gone without a hug, goodbye, or promise to return. Just like that—poof! One day I had a daddy, and the next day I didn't. It wasn't until I was eight or nine that I realized I was supposed to have a father in my life.

One of my fondest childhood memories is sleeping in the same bed with Mom. Our two-bedroom townhouse was the place I remember living after Deddy left. My brother slept in the smaller room. My baby sister and I slept with my mother in the larger bedroom.

My mother was a medium-built, top-heavy woman with shoulder-length black hair and a butterscotch skin tone. She had beautiful white teeth with one gold-trimmed tooth that complimented her big, bright smile and hearty laugh. She was a hardworking woman. I remember her rising early to prepare meals before going to work. I can't remember a time when we didn't have something delicious to eat. She later shared her struggle to keep food on the table and pay the bills, but growing up, I never knew. As far as I was concerned, life was good!

Mom had a mirror on the kitchen wall, near the window, where she would put on her face powder and orange or red lipstick. She was beautiful! I don't remember getting many hugs or kisses or hearing her say, "I love you." I loved her, and I knew she loved me. She ran a tight ship, making it clear that if we didn't like how she did things, we were free to leave. She would say, "You don't have to run away.

Just take your time." She'd even offer to pack us a lunch. She didn't tolerate disrespect.

Mom was a young grandmother at the age of thirty-eight. Most of her grandchildren also called her mom. She was always cracking corny jokes and laughing at them herself. Her hearty laugh would lead others to join her, even when they didn't know why she was laughing. It seemed like she never had a sad day, but that was because she wasn't one to murmur and complain. She took the lemons of life and made lemonade. When people commented on her happy, lively spirit, she shared that her laughter was actually a coping mechanism. Many days, she laughed to keep from crying.

Mom suffered many years of abuse over her twenty years of marriage. I don't remember the abuse myself, but the one time it was mentioned, I asked her why she stayed so long. She said that she was trying to keep the family together. In those days, when you had marital problems—even problems like abuse—your parents would counsel, console, and then send you back home, telling you to work it out. That's exactly what Mom tried to do. She quickly learned that it takes two to have a happy marriage, and she wasn't getting much cooperation. Take note that I said *happy marriage.* So often and for various reasons, a married couple will live in the same house in misery, suffering in a broken relationship. Unfortunately, wearing a wedding ring, changing your last name, or sleeping in the same bed doesn't mean that you're happily married.

When I was about five years old, my oldest sister, my second sister, my oldest brother, and Mom's nephew fell on hard times back-to-back and needed refuge. Mom allowed them and their children to come live with us in our two-bedroom, one-bathroom townhouse. At the time, Mom was the only one working, but with the help of the good Lord, we had plenty of food and were able to meet our basic needs. It was very crowded, but we managed.

# Deddy

My dad, who we called Deddy, was a robust man with hazel eyes that sometimes looked green. He had wavy hair that looked reddish in the sun and a passing skin tone. My only living grandparent, his mother, could pass for Caucasian as well. She had long, beautiful black hair that she always wore in two ponytails parted in the middle, which she wrapped and pinned into knots. She was the best! She loved me and treated me with special hugs and sweet treats, but I often thought within myself that she and my dad *could not* be my people. It's no secret that people of color come in all shades—from deep, dark black to light enough to pass for white. I was darker than my father. There were times when I would be called hurtful names because of the darkness of my skin, which caused me to suffer many insecurities and doubts. I thought that maybe I was adopted, because I rarely saw Deddy and never received phone calls from him. After he left, his name was never mentioned in our house.

I even asked Mom if she would tell me who my "real" parents were. She bucked her eyes, rolling them around with a look that could kill. Before she could speak, I realized that it was not a good question to ask. She scolded me harshly and in a loud voice. I was told to never ask that question again. Mom yelled the fear of God into me that day, and I walked away in total confusion and silence.

The fact that she didn't at least assure me that she was my mother made things even worse. That unpleasant encounter reinforced my feeling of being completely detached from the people around me, like a misfit. I felt like I was alone in this giant world. For the life of me, I couldn't figure out why my question was so offensive or why it never was answered. My younger sister would taunt me sometimes, telling me that I was found on the steps of our back door.

When I was nine years old, Mom introduced me and my siblings to her friend, Mr. Chester. He was a nice man. He'd take us for rides. He'd even buy me and my sister root beer floats and juicy tenderloin sandwiches. Sometimes we would just ride around with no specific place to go, looking at the beautiful scenery.

A couple of months after I turned ten, Mom and Mr. Chester got married. I was super happy because I thought, *at last, I'm going to have a dad.* My brother wasn't too happy. By that time, he was sixteen and marching to his own drumbeat. He wanted to be with Deddy instead of staying with us. My baby sister had a different father than Deddy. She was six and had been without her father all her life. He passed away when she was one or two days old. My sister and I were so in love with Mom that we hadn't given much thought to not having a father around, but we were happy to finally have a dad.

We moved out of our two-bedroom townhouse into a house with three bedrooms. It was an old house that wasn't in the best condition, but we made it work. My sister and I shared a room. Mom was very industrious and would always say, "Take what you've got, and make what you want." She was a master of many things. Once when our vacuum cleaner stopped working, Mom cut the cord and attached a new one. Like magic, it worked until we were able to replace it. Whenever mice found their way into the house, Mom set traps to catch them or swatted and killed them with a broom. She was fearless! I believe that if a bear had come in the house, she would have fought and killed it. There wasn't anything she couldn't or wouldn't do. She encouraged us to always do our best and to do the right thing at all times, even when no one was looking. She taught us to be keepers of our word. Our word was our bond. She made us rise early and get our chores done before going out to play. There was no laziness going on in our house. She would say, "Get up early. Get your chores done, and if you're sleepy, you can always lie down and take a nap later." She led by that example. By ten in the morning, she'd have dinner completed. She would cook dinner while she was cooking breakfast. She wasn't perfect, but she did her best to raise us to be respectable beings.

As for Mr. Chester, he was also a hardworking man. I never knew him to be without work until he retired. When it came to the house, though, he helped with the bills, mowed the lawn, and shoveled snow. When we met him, Mom said we didn't have to call him "Dad," but we couldn't call him "Chester." Back then, children were taught to respect their elders and address them as Mr., Mrs., or Miss. You would get slapped in the mouth for calling an adult by his or her first name. We had to, as she would say, "put a handle on his name," so we called him "Mr. Chester." My baby sister was so in love with him, she fondly called him "Dad." But my brother and I referred to him as Mr. Chester.

About two years later, we moved again, this time to a home my parents purchased. It was less than a mile from our old house, but it was much nicer. We were so proud of our new place. Mom always taught us to take care of what we had, and to keep it clean, as if it cost a million dollars. She would take an old spoon and polish it to look brand new. "If you don't know how to treat secondhand things," she'd tell us, "You surely won't take care of the more expensive."

This period of time was especially significant—a turnaround season for me. It was May 15, 1976, when my mom's sister, Aunt O'Neil, who had just turned forty-nine the month before, suffered a massive stroke and passed away. It was a sad time for our family. I loved when Aunt O'Neil would visit us. She lived in Columbus, Ohio, a little over an hour southwest of Lima, Ohio, where we lived. We called Columbus the "big city," since Lima was a much smaller town of about 38,000 to 40,000 people. She didn't have any children and would always come bearing treats and gifts.

Mom took my baby sister and me with her to Columbus to finalize my aunt's funeral arrangements. While there, many family and friends gathered in my aunt's home, bringing food and drinks to feed our bereaved family. That was the tradition back then. When someone had death in the family, we'd gather around with food, laughter, and hugs to console them. We'd share fond memories of the deceased, and usually the pastor would have prayer with everyone before leaving.

Aunt O'Neil's house was filled with cigarette smoke from those who smoked, and beer cans and liquor bottles from those who drank. I watched and listened to the adults having a gay ole time, smoking and drinking. Mom was asthmatic and didn't smoke or drink, but Mr. Chester did both. I remember stealing a cigarette and a can of beer that someone had left on the table and going upstairs to an empty bedroom. There, I tried to smoke the cigarette and drink the half-cup of beer left in the can. It was the first time I tried to smoke and boy, was it awful! It left me coughing and choking. The beer tasted terrible, too. I couldn't figure out how the adults were down there having so much fun doing these horrible-tasting things. I was so ashamed and didn't want anyone to know what I'd done. If my mom had found out, she would have torn my tail *up* (given me a good ol' fashioned spanking)!

After the funeral, we cleaned out Auntie's house and returned to Lima. Mom took most of the furniture and household belongings. My aunt had beautiful, expensive things and they made our newly purchased home look really nice. Mom kept her bedroom suit until her dying day. Surprisingly, it was still in incredibly good condition.

Shortly after Mom and Mr. Chester married, we started attending a Baptist church. Mom was under conviction to do the right thing by giving God some of her time. After all, the Lord had been good to our family and blessed Mom, helping her get through some hard times. She wanted a closer walk with God for herself and her children. I don't remember my brother going to church, but my baby sister and I had no choice. There, I was baptized in water by the late Pastor Broyles.

I loved going to church. We went to Sunday school and began learning about the Creator of Heaven and Earth. We also learned about Lucifer, once an angel, who was kicked out of heaven because he rose up against the Creator and enticed other angels to do the same. We learned that the first man and woman were Adam and Eve, and that Satan (another name for Lucifer) tricked them into eating the forbidden fruit, causing them to lose their place in the perfect Garden of Eden. As a result, every person born after them was born into the fallen world of sin. I learned that to get back into right standing with the Creator, we needed a blood sacrifice, the only thing that could atone for sin. Jesus Christ was that sacrifice, who died on the old, rugged cross for the sins of the whole world. I was like a sponge and learned so much. That church had many choirs; I started singing in the junior choir, and I remember looking forward to turning eighteen, when I could move on to the young adult choir.

Learning about Creation and going to church was all good. Our new house was pretty, and my family was happy. However, I had reached the point where I wanted Deddy, my father, back in my life. Once a year, he would come to town to visit my grandmother and his siblings. He raised hogs on his farm in North Carolina and would always bring one up with him to have a big hog roast. My aunts, uncles, cousins, and family friends would gather at my grandmother's house and have a boatload of fun, eating, drinking, dancing, and playing games. It was like a big family reunion. Of course, I always wanted to go see him since I never talked to him on the phone or saw him any other time throughout the year. My mother, on the other hand, didn't want me to go, even though I begged her.

One day, however, when I was about eight years old, she finally gave in and allowed me to go see him. When our eyes connected, I ran to him with outstretched arms and he gave me a tight hug and a wet kiss on the cheek and asked, "Who am I?"

I responded, "Deddy!"

He bellowed out a hearty laugh and gave me another tight hug and wet kiss. We were so happy to see one another! I didn't get to spend much one-on-one time with him because he was busy with the hogs and catching up on the latest happenings with his siblings and friends. There was lots of food and fun; alcohol was always a must-have drink during those family gatherings, and Deddy drank his fair share. Although we didn't say much to one another, it was simply good to see him. When it was time to say goodbye, he planted another wet kiss on my cheek. The combination of alcohol and cigarettes on his breath smelled awful, and his sloppy kisses were yucky. I enjoyed the hugs, but I'd wipe the kisses away when I got out of his sight. Nonetheless, I had fun, just knowing I was with him. I would hold onto the memory until the next year.

One summer, several of my nieces and nephews went to spend the summer with Deddy in North Carolina on his hog farm. I wanted to go with them so badly! I begged my mother for weeks, but this time she wouldn't give in. She said, "No, no, no!" I cried and cried and yelled at her angrily, saying, "It's not fair that his grandchildren can go for the summer, but I'm not allowed to go see and spend time with my own father!" I was angry with her for the entire summer, knowing they were down there having fun without me. They had fun all right, but not without their fair share of chores on the hog farm. When they returned, they didn't speak well of those hog chores, but I envied their stories of all the other fun things they did. It made me mad all over again. I just couldn't believe my mother would be so mean.

# Cousin Faye

My mom's niece, my cousin Faye, was one of the rare few in our family who loved the Lord and lived according to the Bible. The rest of us were churchgoers but didn't quite live God-pleasing lives the rest of the week. We attended worship services out of "duty," but had no real relationship with God. One day, Cousin Faye invited us to be guests at her church. Mom wouldn't go, but she allowed me to go after I attended worship service at our own church. Cousin Faye's church was about two blocks from ours, and lasted a lot longer, so I could go when our service dismissed and still get about three hours of their worship service. Yes, you heard correctly: *three hours!* They would begin at eleven o'clock in the morning and not dismiss until about two or three o'clock in the afternoon.

As I got closer to Cousin Faye's church, I could hear music and singing. It sounded so good, I wanted to run fast to get there. When I stepped inside the church, there was no place to sit because the pews were full. I thought, *what in the world is going on in here?* That worship service was nothing like the one I'd just left. The drums were loud. The organ and piano players were bouncing around on their seats. The people were on their feet clapping, playing tambourines, shouting with loud voices, and dancing around like nothing I'd ever seen. I couldn't believe what I was seeing and hearing; I felt like I was in another world. As I looked around, I noticed that I was among the few who weren't on their feet, clapping and singing. Immediately, I stood and began to clap. After a few minutes, I thought, *hey, I like this!* I loved to pop my fingers and dance to non-praise music; to be able to stand, clap, and dance during worship was right up my alley. I fit right in. I enjoyed this church so much that I started to attend their weekday services, too.

On Wednesday, May 26, 1976, about two months after my twelfth birthday and eleven days after Aunt O'Neil's death, Cousin Faye invited me to attend a mid-week worship service. Mom said yes, and I began preparing way before the service began. Mom had washed my hair the night before, and that morning she pressed it with a hot comb. When my hair gets wet, it curls up to a short afro. Back then, as a child, I didn't wear an afro, so Mom would use a brass comb. She'd place it on the stove burner and before it got too hot, she'd comb through a small section of my hair until it was straight. Mom was so good at this that we called her pressing "bone straight." I hated the process because many times, when she put the hair oil on the small section of hair, it would burn my scalp when she got too close. The process was sometimes painful, but the finished product was worth it: nice, shiny, straight hair. It would last for months until it got wet, or the weather was hot, muggy, or rainy. Then it would transform back to the curly afro. That day, my hair was beautiful when she finished, pressed, and styled into two shiny black braids that hung past my shoulders.

Well, I attended the worship service with Cousin Faye on May 26, and at the end, the pastor asked who would like to give their life to the Lord, to live according to the Bible in order to go to heaven. I didn't totally understand what he was talking about, but I saw others go up; I figured this was something good and I wanted it, too. I stood and was invited to come to the first pew. Shortly afterwards, people began to gather around me, forming a circle. They started singing, clapping, and praising God. As we sang and clapped, we were told to tell the Lord we were sorry for the sins we had committed and to ask the Lord to come into our lives to be our Lord and Savior. I immediately thought about those cigarettes and beer I had stolen and consumed just a few days ago. I began to cry so hard that tears began to drop from my chin. I began to tell the Lord how sorry I was and asked Him to please forgive me. I cried like a newborn baby. Others did the same, while the people around us kept singing and praising the Lord. It was such a beautiful sound in that place with all the praise, worship and sounds of repentance. Even now, it gives me chills. I knew something was going on inside of me. I truly felt like I was being born again, dying from my old sinful nature, to be reborn. I later learned that I *was* being born again born to my new life in Christ Jesus, where old things were passing away and all things were becoming new. This was an awesome, yet overwhelming, experience for a twelve-year-old. I was so excited and happy.

When I returned home, my mom said, "What in the world happened to you?" Not only was I still crying for having accepted Jesus Christ as my Lord and Savior, but my hair was a hot mess. The beautiful, bone-straight hair pressing that she had given me before I went to church was now a confused mess of curly and straight. It had gotten wet from perspiration as I cried, sang, clapped, and praised God. I'm sure it must have been a sight to behold. Not really knowing the condition of my hair, I began telling her about my experience at the church and that Jesus Christ now lived in my heart and I was a newborn creature in Him. I began to tell her what life changes I was going to make. I was so full of unspeakable and unexplainable joy. It was the happiest day of my life—one that I will never forget!

Mom couldn't repress my hair until it had completely dried. The next morning, she sat me in front of the kitchen stove and began to press my hair again. As she pressed, she asked lots of questions about my experience and what had happened at the church. I guess she was trying to figure out how a child goes to a worship service with bone-straight hair and comes home with afro puffs.

As months passed, Mom could see a change in my life. She gave me permission to leave our family church and join the noisy crew at Mt. Olivet. Pastor Webster became my new pastor. I began reading my Bible every day. I had a small, red New Testament (Matthew to Revelation, with the books of Psalms and Proverbs included) that I had gotten from school when I was in fourth or fifth grade. Back then, before it became unpopular in the United States to say the name of Jesus Christ and truly declare "it is in God we trust," I received this Bible from the Gideons. Gideons International was founded July 1, 1899, in Janesville, Wisconsin and is now headquartered in Nashville, Tennessee. Members travel to schools and present free Bibles to any student who wanted one.

> Gideons International is an evangelical Christian association founded in 1899 in Wisconsin. The Gideons' primary activity is distributing copies of the Bible free of charge. This Bible distribution is a worldwide enterprise taking place in around 200 countries, territories, and possessions.[1]

My little red New Testament is tattered, but I still have it. I began praying over my meals, giving thanks to the Lord for food to eat when so many were hungry, and asking the Lord to cleanse the food from any unknown impurities that would harm me. I went to as many prayer meetings and worship services as I could, even walking to get there when necessary.

In 1978, the church purchased a beautiful cathedral on the same street, about two or three blocks away from our new home. It didn't get any better than that. I could get there in a five-minute walk. After that, church became my second home. I loved the worship experience, the people, and the opportunities to exercise my God-given talents. I sang in the choir, worked with the young children

---

[1]   "The Gideons International," Wikipedia.com, accessed October 15, 2020, https://en.wikipedia.org/wiki/The_Gideons_International.

as an assistant teacher, and was appointed president of the Sunday night youth Bible study. I also worked with the youth on a district level and traveled to district and statewide conventions, where I met other young people who also loved the Lord. Life was beautiful! It no longer mattered that my father wasn't in my life. My heavenly Father filled that big hole, and I felt His love overshadow my being. I didn't care if I ever saw Deddy again. It was all good.

I loved the Lord and wanted to do the right thing, even to the point that I thought it was time I started calling my stepfather Dad. When I finally got the nerve, he was as shocked as I was.

"What did you say?" he asked.

"Nothing! Never mind!" I said, and I never called him Dad again, from that point until he passed away in 2008. He was a nice man. He never mistreated me, but it didn't feel natural to call him Dad. I wanted to, but somehow, it felt like a bad word coming out of my mouth. My siblings and I never really bonded with him as a parent; it always felt like we were only my mother's children, and he seemed to sense that, too. Instead of reprimanding us when we did wrong, he'd call my mother and tell her what we did or didn't do. It was annoying for her, because she wouldn't have minded if he *had* reprimanded us—but he never did.

When I was about thirteen years old, my cousin Faye and her family moved directly across the street from our new home. I was so happy! It was heaven on earth! I spent a lot of time at her house, helping her cook and clean while we talked about the Bible and other things. Cousin Faye was like a second mother to me, and we became even closer after I accepted Jesus Christ into my life. She taught me the holy scriptures and was very instrumental in my spiritual growth. When I was missing from my house, Mom could always find me at Cousin Faye's.

Five years had passed since I asked my mother about my "real" parents. She'd asked me never to do so again, and I respected her wishes. However, the older I got, the more troubled I became. It was during my father's family gatherings that I began to notice the darkness of my skin and compare it to the light-skinned tones of my siblings and extended family members. Many of them could "pass," and few were as dark as me. The only dark-skinned people close to me were friends of the family, or those who had married into it.

One day, while I was visiting Cousin Faye, her daughter Denise said she had a secret to tell me, and I wasn't allowed to tell anyone. I quickly agreed, eager for some exciting, top-secret information. Nothing could have prepared me for what she whispered next: "Uncle Carl is not your real father." Carl was Deddy's first name.

Well, well, well...can you imagine that? I was in total shock, but somehow, I was able to keep myself together. I felt in my gut that it had to be the truth, and again I wondered if I was adopted, because I didn't think my mother was my mother, either. I can't remember if I asked Denise then, but somehow I was able to confirm that my mother was, indeed, my "real" mother. Then the million-dollar question became, *who is my real father?* Apparently, Denise didn't know, because she never mentioned his name or admitted to knowing who he was. Shortly after that revelation, Cousin Faye would occasionally ask, "Did your mom mention anything about your dad?"

Instead of asking what was it that mom was supposed to tell me, I'd play it off and say, "No, what happened? Is he sick?"

Cousin Faye would abruptly drop the subject and move on to something else. I wasn't sure if Denise told her mother she'd let the secret slip, but I didn't let on to Cousin Faye that I knew any different. I didn't want to get Denise into trouble, but wow, this was a hard secret to keep, and it weighed on me, particularly when I was with my relatives. They were the only relatives I knew. I now understood why my mom never wanted me to go visit Deddy when he'd come to town, and why she'd never allowed me to spend the summer in North Carolina with him. Everyone called Deddy's mother Babe, and that's what she called all of us. Babe was the only grandparent I knew and loved until my mother married Mr. Chester. I then grew to love his mother, Grandma Rose, as well. Babe loved me as she did all the other grandchildren and never treated me any differently. Now, whenever I saw her, though, I carried the huge burden of knowing the truth, yet having to pretend that nothing had changed.

Later on, I discovered that it wasn't much of a secret at all; apparently everyone in the family knew, except for Denise—and me. And when I say everyone knew, I mean *everyone*, including my siblings. I later found out that my brothers and sisters had begged Mom to tell me because they thought it was her place to do it. She ignored their pleas and continued to hide the truth. It amazes me to this day that no one broke their silence and treated me with love and kindness, as if I were truly blood family. I now understand that blood doesn't really make you family. It's those who genuinely love you. In the meantime, I was a young teen, no longer sure exactly who I was, and with no way to find out. All I could do was wonder if every dark man who crossed my path was my father.

It would be several years before Mom told me the truth.

Of course, I did have a heavenly Father, and He continued to support me. I was definitely "not ashamed of the gospel of Christ;" I was so happy with my newfound joy and peace in accepting Jesus as Lord and Savior that I didn't care who knew it. Some of my friends didn't want to have anything to do with me because of this and began calling me "Holy Roller" and other mean and sarcastic names. It didn't bother me one bit. I stayed happy and found new friends who also loved the Lord. Surprisingly, it was my girlfriends who shunned me; my male friends remained loyal. I always thought boys made better friends than girls. With the girls, there was always some jealousy, confusion, or something messy going on.

My male friends saw the light of Jesus in my life and would often say, "I would love to have you as my girlfriend, but I know I don't have a chance because you're not like other girls that I've been with."

Then I'd say, "You're right about that!"

One of them wouldn't accept my rejection, and he kept after me until I finally gave him my phone number. Boy, oh boy, was that the wrong thing to do! He was bad news from the word go. I should have known better, because my pastor taught us that a believer and non-believer were not to date or marry.

> Be ye not unequally yoked together with unbelievers: for what fellowship hath righteousness with unrighteousness? and what communion hath light with darkness? (2 Corinthians 6:14)

> Can two walk together, except they be agreed? (Amos 3:3)

We stopped dating after a few months of disappointment, and I had to repent for disobeying the scriptures. There weren't many young men my age in our assembly who loved the Lord. The few who were there ended up dating most of us at one point or another, but each of the two or three relationships I was in was disappointing, to say the least. I didn't get off to a good start in the dating arena.

# My Awakening

I loved to write and started pen palling with young people across the country, encouraging them to live for the Lord. I was probably around fourteen or fifteen when I met Evangelist Candies High. She was an older woman from New Jersey who came to our assembly to conduct a revival service. She was very strict, but for some reason, she and I connected. I was on the altar seeking more of the Lord and praying to be filled with the Holy Spirit, and she encouraged me to stand up for the Lord and do the right thing. Somehow, she learned that I was a writer and gave me the names of several young ladies she had met in her evangelistic travels. She wanted me to write and encourage them, and I was more than happy to oblige. Not only did I write them, but I'd write her, too. She'd always write back beautiful letters of encouragement.

In 1980, when I had just turned sixteen, she contacted Mom and asked if I could spend a week of my summer vacation with her in New Jersey. Mom didn't know much about her other than that we wrote each other, and that she was a true woman of faith who loved the Lord, but she gave me permission to go. I waited for summer break with great anticipation, both afraid and excited as I looked forward to going somewhere I had never been before. I had never traveled that far without my parents. I boarded the Greyhound bus and made the sixteen-hour journey to Jersey City, New Jersey. It proved to be the best trip of my life. Instead of staying one week, I believe I ended up staying two or three weeks more

Mother High introduced me to the young people from her assembly and other local assemblies that she attended. She would cook a big breakfast and invite them over to fellowship with me. I have fond memories of that trip. The most memorable was when I had an encounter with the Lord unlike any I had ever experienced before. I woke up one morning to the voice of Mother High crying out to the Lord in prayer, which was something she did every morning. She lived in a very small one-bedroom apartment in an inner-city high-rise, and I slept in her living room on a sofa sleeper. That particular morning, I sat on the side of the sofa sleeper and also began to pray. I sensed the strong presence of the Holy Spirit come over me and I began to weep. I sensed the Lord wanting me to do something, but I wasn't sure what or how to get it done. From my spirit, I said, "Lord, whatever you want me to do, please show me and confirm it in the scriptures." I then opened the Bible and began reading the first scriptures my eyes fell upon: Jeremiah 1, the calling of the prophet Jeremiah. I stumbled over the first few verses because there were names that I struggled to pronounce, but I kept reading. When I got to verse five, I began to weep like a baby.

> Before I formed thee in the belly, I knew thee; and before thou camest forth out of the womb I sanctified thee, and I ordained thee a prophet unto the nations.

> Then said I, ah, Lord God! behold, I cannot speak for I am a child.

> But the Lord said unto me, say not, I am a child: for thou shalt go to all that I shall send thee, and whatsoever I command thee thou shalt speak.

> Be not afraid of their faces: for I am with thee to deliver thee, saith the Lord.

> Then the LORD put forth his hand and touched my
> mouth. And the LORD said unto me, Behold, I have put
> my words in thy mouth.
>
> See, I have this day set thee over the nations and over
> the kingdoms, to root out, and to pull down, and to
> destroy, and to throw down, to build, and to plant.
> (Jeremiah 1:5–10)

What does a sixteen-year-old do with such a powerful confirmation of her calling? I sensed there was only one acceptable response. I said, "Yes Lord," and I cried as I read the passage over and over. Then I heard the Lord speak again to my spirit and say, "Like Abraham, I have called you to New Jersey, away from your family, to show you who you are."

> Now the LORD had said unto Abram, get thee out of thy
> country, and from thy kindred, and from thy father's
> house, unto a land that I will shew thee:
>
> And I will make of thee a great nation, and I will bless
> thee, and make thy name great; and thou shalt be a
> blessing. (Genesis 12:1–2)

For someone who felt like a total misfit, not knowing my real father, and carrying the burden of silence for several years, this brought an overwhelming relief, even though I didn't really know the depth of my "yes." I just knew that the Lord had mad love for me and had a purpose for my life; it didn't matter to Him that I was an illegitimate child. He said he knew me before I was formed in my mother's belly. This meant he knew who my daddy was, and all about my messy arrival, and yet He loved me and wanted to use me for His glory! Amidst my tears, I told the Lord that I'd do whatever He said and go wherever He sent me. Mother High was still in her bedroom, crying out to the Lord. I didn't share this with her. It was a precious encounter, and I relished the moment. I figured, with the Lord loving me like that, who needed a daddy?

Soon after that encounter, Mother High called a few pastors and asked them if I could come to their individual worship services to be a guest speaker for their youth groups. The pastors agreed and off I went. I had no clue what to expect or how to prepare. I just followed the Holy Spirit's lead and shared what I thought He'd placed in my heart. After I finished, the pastors asked the congregants to give me an offering as a token of love and appreciation for my sharing the Word of God with them. I was overwhelmed and taken aback by their response. I ended up with way more money than when I arrived. As my visit drew to a close, my emotions were all over the place. I wanted to go back home, and I wanted to stay.

Of course, I had to go back home. When I returned, I was super excited to share my trip and experience with my mother. She was happy for me and glad she'd allowed me to go. I could hardly wait to share everything with my pastor. He smiled as I shared the details of my encounter with the Lord. He said, "I knew you had a calling on your life when you first came to this ministry at the age of twelve, and thus the reason I appointed and promoted you. Now, I'm glad you know it for yourself." He knew some of the members believed that I was too immature as a young teen, and that my promotion was a mistake, but he had done it anyway. He was cultivating the gifts that he saw in me. Before I could tell the Lord no because I was a child, He already had an answer ready for me in Jeremiah, chapter one, verse seven: "say not, I am a child: for thou shalt go to all that I shall send thee and whatsoever I command thee thou shalt speak."

I had so many exciting things going on in my life, I forgot all about sharing it with my dad. Some family members thought I was too young to be so gung-ho about living a sanctified (holy and set apart from the world) life for the Lord. They thought that, instead of my going to church so much, I should be out enjoying the worldly pleasures of youth. Boy, am I glad I didn't listen to *that* jibber jabber!

As young as I was, I knew that the Lord was restoring my confidence and assuring me that I was not a mistake. My life began thousands of years before my mother met my father, as you see in Jeremiah 1:5. The Lord knew me before I was formed in my mother's belly and sanctified me before my mother gave birth. I was in God's plan all along. He knew the circumstances of my parents' relationship and that a "chocolate drop" would be conceived and later born on March 23, 1964. Wow, who *wouldn't* serve a God like that! He is Yahweh El Ashiyb, the Lord my Restorer! I saw this quotation on Pinterest and am not sure of the author, but it blessed me: "There is absolutely NOTHING God cannot restore and NO thing He cannot redeem." It speaks to my life with a resounding crescendo.

# Graduation

Finally, it was graduation time, and I was super excited for a couple of reasons. The first reason was that, out of a graduating class of over 600, I had been chosen to be one of the speakers during our graduation commencement. I was thrilled, but nervous, knowing I would be speaking before a couple thousand people. Okay, I was shaking in my boots. Second, I was going away to college. Yes, I was leaving home!

To my surprise, when I told my pastor that I was going to be one of the commencement speakers, he said he'd be there. This made me even more nervous, knowing he'd be there in that sea of people. On the other hand, I felt honored that he was willing to miss our Friday night worship service just for me. *That* put a big Kool-Aid smile on my face.

The October before graduation, our pastor called me into his office, saying that he needed to talk to me about something important.

Thinking it was something to do with my church work, I followed him in and took a seat. But instead of details about youth groups or worship, he shared some horrible news: he had cancer, and his doctors had given him about six months to live. Never in my wildest dreams did I expect such devastating news. Overcome with grief, I bawled like a newborn baby.

As the months progressed, our pastor grew weaker and weaker, finally giving up in March of 1982, just two months shy of my graduation. His passing was devastating because he was a father figure to me. He and his wife were wonderful people. He afforded and appointed me to positions in ministry that unnerved the older members, causing some to say I needed to sit down and listen to someone older instead of being the one leading them, that I was too young to be in a leadership role. Little did they know that I felt the same, but my pastor always told me that he saw my potential and he wanted to groom me for my purpose and destiny. What did I know? I was a child. A willing child. Willing to do what I was asked, without question or resistance.

Because I studied accounting in our local vocational school, the pastor's wife asked me to help her balance the books of our ministry's day care center. I was always happy to help. They've both gone on to be with the Lord and to this day, I miss them so much. They were very instrumental in my spiritual growth.

I've concluded that nothing happens by chance. There is a sovereign God who's always been and always will be, who is everywhere and in every space at the same time, who sees all and knows all. There is nothing that goes on in the universe that He didn't already know billions of years before it took place. He orchestrates every encounter for purpose; the good, the bad, and the ugly ones. Nothing goes wasted. The Word of God declares

> And we know that all things work together for good to them that love God, to them who are the called according to his purpose. (Romans 8:28)

I don't understand everything about God, but I know that He's real, and I believe that He has a purpose for each of us.

# Time to Leave

My graduation was epic! I was so nervous that my hands and legs were shaking. I was afraid my shaking was seen by others. My speech said goodbye to yesterday and hello to a bright and promising future. After commencement, family and friends gathered at our home, where Mom had prepared tasty snacks for our enjoyment. I received many cards and gifts. It was awesome, but the time came for me to leave for college.

Before my departure date, my baby sister was shouting for joy. She and I always shared a bedroom. Most of the time, her side of the room was messy, and my side was very neat and organized. I hated sharing a room with her, and she hated sharing with me. Well, her time had come; she could finally spread her mess over the entire bedroom, and she was looking forward to it with great anticipation. There'd be no one there to argue with her, or boss her around. She would finally be free.

During my junior year of high school, I'd accepted the offer to attend International Business College in Fort Wayne, Indiana. It was about an hour northwest of Lima and easily accessible. My plans were to earn my associate degree in accounting, then head west to visit a friend in Colorado Springs, Colorado. I thought that would be a great place to live. I loved to travel and was looking forward to that trip.

Mom, however, was very nervous about my leaving and staying on campus. She counseled with Pastor Webster several months prior, and he suggested that I board with a family from Pastor Dupree's church. For the past three or four years, we fellowshipped with a sister church in Fort Wayne, pastored by Elder Dupree. We traded visits during the pastoral celebrations. Mom took the pastor's advice and made a call to the Duprees. Long story short, the Duprees agreed to take me into their home and Mom was relieved.

On Sunday, August 29, 1982, our church had a big celebration to honor our pastoral leaders. Following tradition as our sister church, Pastor Dupree and his members drove over to help us celebrate. It was a grand time in the Lord! We had a big feast with lots of good food. Following the feast, we enjoyed a worship service with singing, praying, and preaching, and many gave short expressions of appreciation to our pastor and his wife. It was always a great fellowship when Pastor Dupree and his congregation came to town. However, as the celebration started to end, my heart began to race, and I could feel tears welling up in my eyes; our gathering wasn't the only thing coming to an end that day. After the celebration, Pastor Dupree drove his beautiful, shiny black Cadillac to my house to load my belongings. He closed the car's trunk, I gave my last hugs, and said goodbye. By this time, my baby sister and I were sobbing. Perhaps she wasn't as happy to see me go as she'd thought. It was a very emotional departure. We sobbed as if we'd never see one another again. When we drove away, everybody was crying. I believe the Duprees were crying too.

# Home Away from Home

The Duprees were wonderful people. They reminded me so much of Pastor Webster and his wife back in Lima. They welcomed me into their home and right away, I felt like I'd known them all my life. They were raising their six-year-old granddaughter. I don't know if she was so happy to share her grandparents with a stranger, but soon she warmed up and we began to bond. She wasn't so thrilled when I called out her mischievous behavior, though. She would roll her eyes and pout. I told her eye rolling and pouting were not allowed in my presence. She would storm off to Pastor Dupree, her Papa. He'd see her sad face and ask what made her so sad. She wanted to tell on me, but she couldn't because I was always right there, staring at her.

Almost exactly a month after I moved in, Mother Dupree's eyesight failed due to her diabetes. She had a minor accident, and Pastor Dupree took her car keys and forbade her to drive. Prior to this, I had been riding the city bus to and from college. I was enrolled in accelerated courses and was in school most of the day. I had to get up extra early to catch the eight o'clock bus to get to class on time, then scurry out of my last class to catch the three o'clock bus to return home. If I was more than a few minutes late out of the last class, I had to wait another hour for the next bus. With Mother Dupree's vision loss, Pastor Dupree, whom I began calling Papa, offered me her car to go back and forth to campus as long as I drove her where she wanted to go. I couldn't believe it. What a blessing! We ended up being a blessing to one another. I knew this was another divine intervention. Who could have orchestrated this connection with such precision? Nobody but a sovereign God.

With Mother Dupree's sight being limited, I stepped up to help care for their six-year-old granddaughter and took on any household chores that were challenging for Mother Dupree. I kept her granddaughter's hair combed, washed clothes, helped with homework, and made basic meal preparations. I was able to do almost everything with one exception: I couldn't get up enough nerve to give her the insulin shots she needed for her diabetes. Guess who took on that heroic task. Her granddaughter! Yes, the six-year-old! I would load the needles, and her granddaughter would give her a shot in the arm, stomach, or thigh. Learning about diabetes was a rude awakening for me. When I was younger, I'd hear people refer to it as "Sugar." They'd say, "Mr. Bluebird's sugar was out of control." It wasn't until I lived with the Duprees that I understood that diabetes and "sugar" were one and the same, and how serious it could be. Boy, did I learn and take on a lot in a short period of time. School was stressful, but with the Lord's help, I managed.

# Man Meets Girl

The Duprees had a thriving ministry with lots of young people. They were known for their Friday night fellowships. They had a worship service every Friday night and afterwards, the young people would gather at someone's home for games and fun or gather at the twenty-four-hour Azar's restaurant. This wasn't something I was accustomed to at my home church. It was fun, and I got a chance to meet and mingle with new friends.

In February of 1983, one of those new friends had a birthday party after a Friday night worship service. All the young people who attended the worship service met in her basement for games and food. Everyone was having a great time except one lonely young man who was sitting and eating by himself. My friendly self and I walked over and asked his name.

"Michael," he said.

Then I told him my name. I asked him why he was sitting by himself and invited him to join the rest of the gang in fun and games. He turned down that offer, so I stayed and talked to him, hoping to help him feel included and not alone in a noisy and crowded basement full of young people. I don't remember the conversation, but we laughed and talked the time away. I do remember that he had recently given his life to the Lord and was becoming acclimated to his new life as a follower of Jesus. That consisted of making new friends with like-minded believers. Though he grew up in this church, he wasn't friends with the young people; when he turned eighteen, he stopped attending, rebelling against his mother, who required him to attend against his will. You know, for many kids, it was fun going to church before they became teenagers. Then all of a sudden, it wasn't the cool thing to do. You didn't want your friends to know you were a "church boy" or "church girl" because they'd make fun of you. Back then, the born-again parents would say, "As long as you live in *this* house, you're going to church…like it or not!" For about seven years, Michael did his own thing: smoking, drinking, getting high, and whatever else he chose as worldly pleasures.

I hadn't officially joined the church in Fort Wayne, but they allowed me to participate as a member. Back then, we called it a "watch care membership." That's when you weren't a member, but the pastor and members treated you like you were until you returned to your own church. They looked out for you and served as points of accountability. Mother Dupree was one of the church's organists and often times played for the choir. Her eyesight may have been failing, but she made beautiful music on those piano and organ keys. The Duprees were thought of highly in the community, and her talent was well known throughout the city. She encouraged me to join the choir, so I did. Mother Dupree played the organ and Mother Payton, Michael's mom, was the president of the choir. She was a sweet lady who was very soft-spoken and well-respected.

I remember once that Mother Dupree purchased some soft-smelling perfume and gifted it to me. It was her way of saying that the strongly scented perfume that I was wearing (Timeless by Avon) was too much for a young eighteen-year-old. Not knowing her intentions, I received it gladly. Later she told me why she bought me that perfume. By then, I had to agree with her. I hadn't known any better; I just thought it smelled good. No one had told me anything different. Looking back, I'm sure others probably talked about me, but only Mother Dupree loved me enough to tell me the truth. You gotta love her for it! She was a wise woman, and I learned so much from her.

One day, the house phone rang, and Mother Dupree answered it. I could vaguely hear her side of the conversation—things like, "Well, hello there! What a pleasant surprise! What brings you to making this call? Sure you can, I don't mind, if she doesn't." I didn't pay much attention. When she hung up, though, she turned to me. "That was Brother Michael. He was asking permission to call you sometime and I told him sure, if you didn't mind."

I'd never had *that* happen before. Normally, when a guy wanted to call me, he would just ask me directly for my phone number. I was used to having male friends and thought Michael was a nice guy. So sure, I was willing to talk to him sometime. I believe he called me the next day, and the rest is history! Michael was and is a kind and very soft-spoken gentleman. He is the eleventh of twelve children; his father passed away when he was two months short of being three years old. Our first date was to Wendy's for fast food burgers.

Michael first called me in early 1983. We became engaged that September and were married in December. As I'm writing this book in 2020, by the grace of God, we will celebrate our thirty-seventh anniversary. Some might think our relationship moved very quickly, but we didn't have a long courtship because we were taught from the scriptures

> But if they cannot contain, let them marry for it is better
> to marry than to burn. (1 Corinthians 7:9)

We were burning up, so it was best for us to marry, rather than to continue to burn with sexual desire. Michael was six years older than me, and ready to settle down. I was a young kid, so I didn't know if I was ready or not, but I said yes to his proposal, and no one tried to talk me out of it. Our wedding day was the coldest day of the year with sub-zero temperatures. It was so cold that the highways were closed. Only medical vehicles were allowed on the streets.

Sadly, Mother Dupree's health had drastically declined due to complications from her diabetes, and she passed away in October of 1983, which meant she wasn't able to celebrate my college graduation or our wedding. I still miss her so much! But now Mother Payton had me as a new daughter-in-law and took over where Mother Dupree left off. Her grandchildren fondly called her Dear. She, too, was a wise woman and taught me many things. She taught me how to be a wife to her son and a mother to our baby girl, Asia. Michael, Jr. was born a little over two years later. My children are my pride and joy. They gave me hope to keep pressing through the hard times that were to come. At this point, life was moving at lightning speed, but it was good, and we were happy.

# He Passed Away

We lived with Mother Payton when we first married. Less than two weeks after our wedding, I received a call from one of my siblings, who told me that Deddy had passed away. I'm not sure what I said in response, but I didn't have any emotions one way or the other. It was like being notified that a stranger had died. I ended up sharing with my husband that I didn't know who my real father was, and that I thought I was adopted. He admitted that I didn't resemble anyone in my family. By this time, my hair was turning grey. I had a white streak down the middle, like a skunk patch. I couldn't believe it. I'd had a few grey strings since I was fifteen or sixteen, but it wasn't very noticeable. Now, it was growing wild with grey and no one else in my family had hair like mine. My husband and I talked about hiring a private investigator to help me find my father, but we figured it would be costly and neither of us had money for that. We needed to be focused on saving money to find our own apartment. Sometime after though, the Lord comforted me by letting me know He was going to help me find my dad, and it wasn't going to cost me a dime. The excitement was overwhelming! I just needed to be patient, and to wait on Him.

I didn't have to wait very long. A few months after Deddy died, my husband and I took a trip to Lima to visit with Mom. While we were there, she unveiled some deep, dark secrets. They were the missing pieces to the secret my cousin Denise forbade me to share six years prior.

# Woman Meets Man

Mom called me into a private upstairs bedroom and told me that she was sorry that I had gone all those years thinking Deddy was my father. She told me that they had separated after Deddy threatened her at gunpoint. She was afraid and escaped to Dayton, Ohio to live with a friend. She was fed up with Deddy and his shenanigans and was determined to leave him. While in Dayton, at a bar, she met George, whom everyone called G. He was G.W. She said he was in the military, was good-looking with long sideburns, and was very kind. They talked and had a good time and continued to see each other. After I don't know how many dates, they "hooked up" and became intimate with one another. She soon discovered she was pregnant. Yes, that's what happens when you have unprotected sex; the chance of getting pregnant significantly increases. That didn't go over well with G.W. because he was going to be discharged from the military soon and would be heading back to New York. When Mom told him she was pregnant, he asked if she would go with him. She wasn't able to do that because she had left my five-year-old brother behind in Lima to finish school and had planned to go back to get him once the school year ended. She didn't know G.W. that well and didn't think going to New York would be a good idea. She declined.

When school was out, G.W. took Mom back to Lima to get my brother and some belongings so that she could settle in Dayton.

# No, She Didn't. Yes, She Did

After some time passed, Deddy began calling Mom, begging her to come back to Lima. She finally told him that she wasn't going back because she was pregnant, and that the baby was not his. He was desperate to have her back and told her he didn't care if she was pregnant; he would raise the baby as if it were his own. Finally, after struggling to make it in Dayton with minimal education and working penny-ante jobs, she relented and moved back. Yes, she did.

All seemed to be well until I was born. Then, things started to go topsy-turvy. When Deddy's friends and other family members saw "his" new baby, they'd say, "Man, you know that chocolate baby ain't yours!" Of course, that played with his ego and made him feel some type of way. Because it was so obvious that I wasn't his child, he went back to mistreating Mom, so badly that they eventually separated again. This time, he left and never came back.

Mom was relieved, but she felt terrible about the position this put me, her daughter, in. She was sad that she couldn't just call my dad, G.W., on the phone and let me speak to him. All she had were a few letters that he'd written, but she couldn't find them. The only thing she knew in addition to his name was that the postmark from his letters was from Mount Vernon, New York.

I asked why she was just now telling me after nineteen years. She said it was because one of the conditions of her returning to Deddy was that, as long as he lived, she was never to tell me that he wasn't my father. *Wow!* I was speechless. Well, Deddy had passed away, and now I knew the whole story. I didn't know what to say. We just sat there in silence for a while. She said that for those whole nineteen years, she'd been tormented with not being able to tell me the truth, and it became even more painful for her when I started asking who my real parents were. She prayed to the Lord that nothing would happen to her before she could tell me the truth. She believed she owed me that much. You see, Mom had a bad case of bronchial asthma, and we thought each asthma attack would be her last one. My baby sister and I would sit terrified in the car as Mr. Chester sped across town, taking her to the emergency room to get help because she couldn't breathe. Her wheezing would get louder and louder the closer we got to the hospital, while my sister and I cried our eyes out in the back seat. I'm sure she thought every ride would be her last.

Carrying a nineteen-year-old burden and suffering with asthma, it's a miracle that Mom lived ninety-four years. God rest her sweet soul! I gained a newfound respect for her strength and courage that day. She could have given me away or aborted me. She had options, but she chose to keep me and endure the shame. She watched me grow up and get married, and still had to keep her promise to keep her secret. God heard her prayers and relieved her burden. But now she had a new prayer: "Lord, let her find her father before I die."

# Moving On, Up, and Out

After living with Mother Payton for a while, Michael and I moved into our own apartment with our clothes, a bedroom set, and a few odds and ends. We didn't have much, but we were happy. We adjusted and made do with what we had until we could do better. I could hear my mother's voice saying, "You have to crawl before you can walk." It seemed that we were doing belly flops sometimes, instead of crawling, but things worked out.

Not long after the move, our beautiful baby girl was born. She was a lovely, happy bundle of joy. She made us proud. Her delivery was horrific, however. I was in labor for fourteen and a half hours and ended up having an emergency C-section. I then contracted some kind of infection and was very sick. I ended up spending two weeks in the hospital.

It was great to be able to stay home and bond with my baby girl, but after about seven months, I decided to find a job to help out with our expenses. The nice thing about my going back to work was that my husband worked seconds or thirds and was able to care for our baby girl while I worked first shift.

In January 1986, in my quiet time of prayer, I heard the Lord speak to my spirit from Isaiah 43:18–19:

Remember ye not the former things, neither consider the things of old.

Behold, I will do a new thing; now it shall spring forth; shall ye not know it? I will even make a way in the wilderness, and rivers in the desert.

I didn't know the depth of the interpretation, but it sounded good, and I was excited. I'd figured, anything new was worth the wait.

The very next month, I found out I was pregnant. We were excited to have another child. We wished for a boy, since we already had a girl. I thought to myself, that a baby was a new thing, and maybe that's what God was trying to tell me.

I was wrong.

# Drifting Away

Before our second child was born, Michael had begun to slacken in his walk with the Lord. He started skipping church. He picked up some of his old habits and began drinking, smoking, and using marijuana. He seemed to drift away, right before my eyes. I was very disappointed; I hadn't planned on being married to someone like that. I thought to myself, *this doesn't line up with the scripture the Lord gave me.* These changes in his life caused stress in our marriage, but we still made it work. He loved me and the children, I loved him… and we worked through it. We were so excited and thankful for the birth of our new baby boy, Michael Jr. The joy of having our two children helped to smooth over our differences. Life wasn't as good as I'd hoped, but it wasn't all bad.

I tried not to badger Michael about us being unequally yoked, but it was stressful and challenging. I didn't want to beat him up and nag him about his broken relationship with the Lord, because I thought it might drive him farther away. However, I did tell him, "If you leave the Lord, you're going to have to deal with seven more devils. This time in your life will become worse than it ever has, and nothing you do is going to make it better until you turn back to the Lord." He just rolled his eyes at me and continued on doing whatever it was he was doing. But I knew what I was talking about:

"When the unclean spirit is gone out of a man, he walketh through dry places, seeking rest, and findeth none.

Then he saith, I will return into my house from whence I came out; and when he is come, he findeth it empty, swept, and garnished.

Then goeth he, and taketh with himself seven other spirits more wicked than himself, and they enter in and dwell there: and the last state of that man is worse than the first. Even so shall it be also unto this wicked generation." (Matthew 12:43–45)

# The Big Bang

We had already moved a couple of times before our son was born, but two weeks after his arrival, we purchased our first home. It was bittersweet. We were excited to finally be homeowners, but I had just had a new baby by C-section and my activities were restricted during my healing process. My sister friend, Vee, was a godsend. She helped us unpack and put things away. What a blessing!

Our new home was lovely. It had been totally gutted and remodeled; everything was new. It was nice and spacious, and everyone had his or her own bedroom. Life was good.

We made it through 1986 and 1987…and then came 1988. Oh my! It was the most challenging time of our five-year marriage, and of my life. My husband says he was "tricked," but whatever the case, it turned out to be a horrifying trick. Life wasn't so good anymore. In fact, to say it was *very* bad would be an understatement.

Suddenly, we were short of money. Sometimes it seemed to just disappear, without any explanation. I couldn't figure out for the life of me what was going on. Then one day, during my quiet time of prayer, the Lord revealed what was *really* happening. While cleaning out the coat closet, I found a tiny zip-lock bag on the floor. I picked it up and saw something in it that looked like white chalk or flour. In my bewilderment, I heard the Holy Spirit say, "It's crack cocaine." It took my breath away. Crack cocaine? I had never seen crack before, how could this be? I wanted to storm out and beat my husband with a baseball bat. I was furious that he'd do this to our family. But in my rage, the Holy Spirit calmed me and said, "Be still, don't say a word!" *What? Be still?* You mean I have another secret that I can't reveal? This couldn't be happening. I was overwhelmed by secrets, with no one to talk to. As hard as it was, however, I pulled myself together, held my peace, and moved along like nothing had ever happened in the coat closet.

# The Truth

I don't remember how much time passed, but it wasn't very long after the coat closet experience. We were lying in bed one night and Michael told me that he had a secret he'd wanted to share with me for a while but was afraid to. The Holy Spirit had already prepared me, so I responded, "I already know."

He said, "No, you don't. This is *really* bad."

Again, I responded, "I already know."

He asked, "How do you know?" I told him about the coat closet experience, and he began to sob uncontrollably. He begged my forgiveness and said he was so sorry—that he didn't mean for this to happen, that he'd been tricked. He explained that when he had gone to a drug house to purchase marijuana, they gave him crack instead. He knew what to do with it, so he smoked it and got hooked on the first puff. He said the first high was unlike any high he'd ever had, and the chase began. He said this addiction was stronger than any other. He was spinning out of control; he wanted to quit, but he couldn't.

# The Great Loss

We talked about all that had happened, and the damage that had already been done because of his drug use. He apologized, and we moved on. I naively thought life would be good again.

In a few short weeks, however, things quickly began to go south. We didn't have money to pay our bills and started receiving disconnect notices. Household appliances and items were coming up missing and our checking account was in the negative. I was scared and didn't know what to do. It was depressing to watch all that we'd worked so hard for go down the drain in a matter of no time. The loss was great. I felt so hopeless and helpless.

I began panning the congregation in hopes of finding someone to talk to, someone who could relate and help me through this nightmare. I came up with a big, fat zero. I had never heard anyone mention that he or she was ever on drugs or married to a drug addict. I don't recall hearing many sermons preached or teachings to the young ladies about coping with addictions. I was in panic mode. I was too ashamed to go to Mom, my siblings, family members, or even a friend. I was a young twenty-three-year-old, with a not quite four-year-old and a fifteen-month-old. What in the world had I gotten myself into? What did I say "I do" to? *I, Anita, take you, Michael, to be my lawfully wedded husband, to have and to hold from this day forward, for better, for worse, for richer, for poorer, in sickness and in health, until death do us part.* Wow, who pays attention to these vows anyway? Who could know exactly what they are signing up for and promising to do for a lifetime? "Til death?" Oh my! *It couldn't get any worse*, I thought. *We couldn't get any poorer*, I thought. We had fallen lower than the bottom, and this was *not* what I'd signed up for. I thought, *I'm better than this. I don't have to take this!* But with no money to pay bills or buy food and a negative bank balance, what was I to do?

Thankfully, Michael still had a job, and a good one at that. Paydays were dreadful. He would be paid on Friday and be broke on Friday night. At one point, he told me that someone had stolen his wallet. He made up all kinds of lies. Before the coat closet experience, I had believed most of them, but now there were so many that I became cynical. I threatened to leave him, but he would say, "You wouldn't be able to make it without me." Wow, why did he say that? I could feel my blood start to boil. That sounded like a dare. I thought, *I don't need you; I can show you better than I can tell you.* I had heard Mom say that during some of her angry moments. Not having money to pay bills or buy food had begun to beat me down.

In my frustration, I took matters into my own hands, packed up all of my husband's clothes, and put them on the back porch. When he came home, several big black garbage bags met him at the back door. He did not resist. He knew he was wrong. He took them and put them in the trunk of his car. I thought, *I'm not putting up with this, I can do bad all by myself!*

In my rage, I heard the Holy Spirit speak to my spirit, in a still small voice, "Whatever you do, you're not allowed to get a divorce."

In a loud voice, I said, *"What,* Really Lord! You mean I have to stay married to a drug addict?"

What do you do when you don't know what to do?

> In my distress I cried unto the LORD, and he heard me.
> (Psalm 120:1)

I was backed into a tight corner with no one to talk to. I had no choice but to go to the only One who knew this was going to happen, billions of years before Michael and I were born. I figured if God knew it was going to happen, He must know when it was going to end, and what I needed to do until it ended.

# Prayer Mode

Mind you, I was still going to work every day, and now I was raising two little ones by myself—or should I say, without my husband. I wasn't truly by myself because I had surrendered my will to fight and given this battle to the Lord. He promised to never leave or forsake me (Hebrews 13:5).

With all that was going on, I still managed to be faithful in attending worship services, prayer meetings, and Bible study, and to manage the business of the church. In addition to working and caring for young toddlers, I became the church's administrator, which carried great responsibilities, such as keeping track of all the finances and business of the ministry. On the floor, with my face down, I began to cry out in prayer for direction. My children and I were on our knees at the hour of prayer. I was desperate for a breakthrough. I needed the Lord to be our provider, protector, and director.

I was in prayer mode all during the day asking if I could or should do this or that. It had gotten to the point that I prayed about what food to purchase. I had to use wisdom and buy foods that could stretch until I had the money to purchase more. I had applied for welfare but was denied because I earned a few dollars over the income guidelines. To this day, I do not understand how they could deny a struggling single mother food and a little help. I figured I was a taxpaying citizen and should be entitled to *some* help during hard times. But I received nothing. I remember hearing the Holy Spirit say, "I'll feed you." I cried so much during those dark days that I did not think I had any tears left to cry. Since I could not divorce, I needed the Holy Spirit to tell me what to do to get through. I would tell the Lord what I was about to do, and said that if He disapproved, I needed Him to block it before I proceeded. The first thing I heard the Spirit say was that I should close the bank account and open a new one without my husband's name on it. He told me to keep giving a tithe (10 percent of my income), because it was going to be the link to my financial breakthrough. I was willing to do this because it wasn't much and, given the amount of debt I had hanging over my head, that little tithe wasn't going to make a down payment on anything.

# Take His Money

Before I packed up Michael's clothes, I told the Lord that I was going to do it and He should block it if He did not agree. I felt like I was blindfolded, feeling my way through the dark. I was totally dependent on the Lord's guidance.

Even with me working, things were still going downhill; I did not make enough to pay bills, a mortgage, and buy groceries, much less pay for childcare. When Michael left, he promised to give me money to help with food and to pay the babysitter. Well, if you have ever heard the lies of an addict, you know that was not going to happen—and it didn't. I did not see one red cent.

Again I turned to prayer. I told the Lord what I was about to do, and asked that, if He (the Lord) did not agree, He would block it. If my husband was not going to give me money, I had to *take* his money. I consulted a lawyer to find out how I could have his wages garnished, since he was blowing the entire check anyway. Mr. Bluebird was a family court judge, and I figured he would be sympathetic to my situation. The only way I could get money, however, was to file for a legal separation. It was not a divorce, and the Lord did not block me, so I moved forward. I paid my $250.00, shared my pitiful story, and to my surprise, the judge scolded *me* (as if he knew me personally). The nerve of him! He said, in a nice/nasty tone, "Why would you want to stay with someone like that? For $200 more, I can file your divorce and you can move on with your life."

I could not believe my ears. There I was before a family court judge, and he was encouraging me to break up my home. Well, it was already broken into a big mess, but I didn't need him to agree and speak so harshly. I felt my blood boil and tears welling up in my eyes. If I hadn't so desperately needed the money, I would have stormed out of his office and slammed the door off the hinges. Even now, just remembering, I'm starting to feel hot with anger. Lord, give me the grace to continue! I was emphatic about why I was there and asked the judge to do as I had requested and paid him to do. He could see how upset I was and proceeded with no more argument. He told me when I should expect the first payment, and I was on my way. Whew, what a relief! I felt like I was in the fiery furnace in that office, with no way of escape.

Well, well, well. To my surprise, the judge wasn't the only one who thought I should divorce. When the church members started to find out what was going on, some of them also advised me to end my marriage. Some went so far as to say, "God hates divorce, but I believe you're not bound to the marriage because of abandonment."

> For the LORD, the God of Israel, saith that he hateth putting away: for one covereth violence with his garment, saith the LORD of hosts: therefore, take heed to your spirit, that ye deal not treacherously. (Malachi 2:16 KJV)

> "I hate divorce," says the GOD of Israel. GOD-of-the-Angel-Armies says, "I hate the violent dismembering of the 'one flesh' of marriage." So, watch yourselves. Don't let your guard down. Don't cheat. (Malachi 2:16 MSG)

> "For I hate divorce!" says the LORD, the God of Israel. "To divorce your wife is to overwhelm her with cruelty," says the LORD of Heaven's Armies. "So, guard your heart; do not be unfaithful to your wife." (Malachi 2:16 NLT)

At that time, I didn't know these scriptures were in the Bible, but I knew that my brethren's advice wasn't coming from the Lord, because He'd clearly told me *not* to divorce. Besides, my husband hadn't abandoned us; I'd put him out. I believe some church people were genuinely trying to help, but some were just anticipating the demise of our marriage because it gave them some drama to gossip about. This was just like the devil, whose assignment is to steal, kill, and destroy (paraphrased from John 10:10a).

Just like the judge said, in about two weeks, I received my first child support check, and it was over $300. I thought, *wow, this can't be right.* Yes, it *was* right and was going to "be right" at that same amount every week. *Blessed be God,* I thought, *I should have done that months ago!*

Well, you probably already know what happened next. Later that evening, after he got off work, Michael stormed over to the house in a rage, totally out of character for him because, by nature, he is pretty laid-back and very mild-mannered. That night, I learned that when you start messing with people's money, they can quickly come unglued. You don't mess with a man's money. Michael complained that he didn't have money to "live on." I had no sympathy for him because he, God, the devil, and I knew he wasn't "living" on that paycheck; he was using it all for drugs. He wasn't paying rent for shelter because he was sleeping in his car. Oh boy, was that man in a hot mess, literally. That summer was blazing hot, with record-breaking heat indexes, and if there was any breeze blowing at all, it was a hot and muggy one. It was a bad summer to be homeless, but all he cared about was getting his next high.

# The Crack House

With less money to spend on drugs, Michael got desperate and started stealing and doing whatever it took to get his next fix. It was so bad, he ended up pawning his car for drugs, and eventually selling it for about six or seven crack rocks. He didn't even own the car. He was still making payments on it. Who does that? A feening (drug craving) addict does that. Not only did he lose his car, but he also forgot to get his clothes out of the trunk before selling it to the drug dealer. There he was: homeless, carless, with literally nothing but the clothes on his back. And what do you do when your car shelter is gone? You start sleeping *in the crack house*. Yes, that was his new home: no specific address, just wherever he was allowed to stay.

This was all way out of my league. I had never been around drugs or seen anything like this horror story. I definitely didn't plan on this being my happily ever after. He'd come by to see the children and ask for a plate of food and a cold glass of water to drink, but I wouldn't give him a crumb. I told him, "You blew the opportunity to eat a plate of food and maybe eat seconds. You had running water to drink all day, every day, but you chose drugs; therefore, wherever you were before this visit, return there to get a plate of food and a cold glass of water." I said what I meant and meant what I said.

He couldn't believe his ears. "I thought you were such a Christian," he sneered.

I wasn't going to take that. "I'm saved, sanctified, and filled up with the Holy Ghost," I replied, "But you're not coming back up in here, eating or drinking anything that you didn't bring with you."

# I See Daylight

Things were looking up for me and the children because we had been getting some nice support checks. I was able to buy complete meals and get the utility bills caught up. I was beginning to see daylight. What a relief!

On the other hand, things continued to go downhill for my husband. He was about to lose his job. Before they let him go, his manager counseled with him and offered him a leave of absence if he would go into treatment. He agreed and went through the Washington House drug treatment program.

He completed the program and went back to work, clean and sober. Praise God! It was a wonderful blessing to have his employer show such kindness. They said he was a hard worker and they wanted to do everything they could to help him. I couldn't help but be optimistic. Perhaps things were going to start getting better again. Perhaps we'd eventually be able to put these trials behind us.

# Here We Go Again

I was naïve. It had been two weeks since Michael had gone back to work, and payday was on the horizon. To my surprise, he spent the entire check (at least, what was left after the support was taken out) on crack. Yes, he did. Back to the crack house he went. I was dumbfounded, to say the least.

Eventually, his employer found out he had relapsed. In another effort to help him, they allowed him to go through treatment again, this time to St. Joseph's Koala Treatment Center. Again, he got clean and stayed clean—until payday. Then it was back to the crack house. The Washington House and Koala Center were short-term treatment centers. Apparently, they were not enough. As for me, I would go to his NA (Narcotics Anonymous) meetings as family support and listen to all the horrific stories of addiction and how it was destroying families and friendships. I thought I had a ragged story, until I heard other addicts tell theirs. It made our story sound like "The Four Little Bears." These people were in six-figure debt, had lost their multi-million-dollar businesses, divorced more than once, lost custody of their children, went bankrupt, tried to commit suicide (some more than once)...and the stories went on and on. I would cry so much, my head ached. I just could not do it anymore. I was so stressed, *I* was beginning to look like I was smoking crack. People had begun asking how I was losing the weight. Believe you me, I needed to lose weight after having two babies, but not in that manner.

Michael's employer even paid for him to see a psychiatrist. I went with him for support. I could not believe that doctor was being paid. As part of his therapy, he instructed Michael to hold a coin in his fist while he slept at night. If he was still holding it when he awakened in the morning, he had a better chance of staying sober. The coin was supposed to represent his sobriety. Who ever heard of such silliness? I thought, *I'm not the brightest bulb in the socket, but that didn't make any sense whatsoever. Who sleeps at night without eventually relaxing their hands?* I refused to go to any more of those sessions with him. Nothing was working.

Finally, my husband's employer allowed him a leave for more extensive treatment. The children and I drove him two hours south of Fort Wayne to the Richmond State Hospital. It was a difficult two-hour ride. By this time, I had lost all faith in Michael's recovery. For a short time before his check-in, he and I sat at the picnic table and talked about the next steps while the children played in the grass. He was sobbing and so was I. Just when I thought I had cried my last tear, more came, and they kept coming and coming. He rose to say goodbye, gave us hugs, and then took the long walk to the entrance to check in. The children never had a clue; they were too young to understand what was happening. When they noticed that Dad had stopped returning home from work, they would ask about him, but I would tell them, "He's gone" or "He'll be back later." Anything to pacify their curiosity yet keep them in the dark about what was really happening to their family.

I felt like we were saying goodbye for the very last time, and that we would never see each other again. I believe I cried all the long drive home. When we got in the house, I cooked and cried, I washed dishes and cried, I put the children to bed and cried. I cried myself to sleep. All through the night, I could hear myself sniffing and sighing from the tears. The next morning, I felt like I had been working on the railroad all the livelong day. I was so tired. I was physically, mentally, and emotionally exhausted.

# No Contact

During the ninety-day program at Richmond, Michael wasn't allowed to make any calls or have visitors for the first two weeks. They had a no contact rule in place to give the patients time to acclimate to the rules and regulations of the sobriety program, without outside distractions or influences.

I was good with that rule, but it was hard on him, and on the children. The children kept asking about him. I told them, "Daddy's sick and had to go get some help to make him feel better again. We'll go to see him soon." When he was finally allowed to have visitors, the children and I packed up my little Escort and headed south to Richmond, where we were able to spend two hours with Michael. I packed a picnic and he and I sat at that same picnic table we had been at just a few weeks ago. The children had fun playing in the grass. We ate lunch and had a great visit. Every weekend, the children and I would make that two-hour drive, until his final day in the program came, and he was released to come home.

# Back Home

Michael looked so good, and we were feeling very hopeful, since he was able to do ninety days of treatment instead of thirty. He was talking with a level head and promised to man up and take over his responsibilities to the family. I was relieved and scared, all at the same time.

During the two-hour ride back to Fort Wayne, he asked to come *back home*. I was afraid to say yes, for fear he'd mess up again, and afraid to say no, for fear he'd go back to drugs since he hadn't had a "real" place to call home since I'd put him out. Despite all of my fear, I hesitantly said, "Yes." My blood started heating up again. I was so afraid; I wanted to change my mind and say no. Nevertheless, I thought, I'd give him another chance. I'd surely want someone to be merciful to me and give me one.

Before I knew it, we were home. That two-hour ride seemed awfully short—way shorter than it had been three months ago. We unloaded his belongings, which were very few, and headed inside. The children were so happy. They jumped and climbed all over him. I cooked a meal, we ate, laughed, and life was good again. It was good to have my husband *back home*.

# Unemployed

He went back to work, and all was lovely. I was still getting child support and he agreed to give me the balance of his check. Our days were normal again, and Michael seemed to be staying sober. Life was starting to improve, and I dared to hope that we were past the worst of it.

The one day, out of nowhere, he came home from work and told me he was fired.

*"Fired!"* I shouted. "For what reason?"

He said he had a dirty drop, and his employer had to let him go. A dirty drop? How in the world do you have a dirty drop when I have all the money? Well, I learned a new lesson that day: you don't necessarily need money to get high. Other addicts are willing to share, and your drug dealer can give you drugs on loan. Wow, you could have knocked me over with a feather. I was past dumbfounded. There were no words to describe how I felt at that moment. Now we were even worse off than we had been before because no job meant no child support, no anything.

# Back to Mom's

We tried to move on together anyway, but one day we got into a big argument about his addiction. I will never forget that day. It was Sunday, October 9, 1988, Mom's sixty-third birthday. I called my friend Vee and her husband to come over because I was afraid Michael was going to fight me physically, which he'd never done before. I was trying to put him out again, but this time, he wasn't willing to leave. I was sobbing, the children were crying. They didn't know what in the world was going on. I had to call the police.

When the officer came and heard our story, he said, "One of you will have to leave." I thought, *not me, I have two small children.* Michael still refused, though, so I called Mom, sobbing on the phone to ask if I could come back home. This was a complete shock to my mother, because this was the first time she had heard of my husband's drug use. She was livid. She began yelling at him and threatened to hurt him if he laid any hands on me. I tried to assure her that he was not fighting me and had not physically hurt me, but she was in such a rage, she heard nothing I said. My friends helped me pack my small Escort with all our clothes and off to Lima I drove, down Highway 30, bawling like a baby.

Our lives were now a total mess. I moved back home with Mom because she had always told us, "If you leave home right, you can come back," by which she meant leaving in a respectable manner. I didn't know of anywhere else I could go with two small children. I was young and immature. I didn't know then about shelters for women and children. I didn't ask anyone in Fort Wayne for help; when some found out I had to move back to Ohio, they didn't offer to help me. Without housing options, I headed to Lima, not thinking about my job being in Fort Wayne. Oh me, oh my! That Monday morning, I called my boss and explained my dilemma; in her compassion, she gave me a week off so I could get myself together. I was relieved and thankful. I needed some time to gather myself and my thoughts.

It was, oddly enough, a good week. I had a chance to share my drama with Mom. She couldn't believe her ears and asked why I hadn't told her before then. I told her I was hoping, every day, that things would get better and besides, I was so ashamed to be in this situation. Not only was I ashamed, but my heart was filling with hatred. I hated my husband for what he'd done to our family. Just the mention of his name made my blood boil. I was mad with the Lord for not allowing me to get a divorce; at that point, I was willing to live the rest of my life alone, separated from the man I'd married, knowing I'd never be able to find or marry anyone else. I just wanted out.

That night, as I went to bed in the house I'd left as a new college girl so long ago, I realized what day it was. I'd ruined Mom's birthday with all my drama. I don't even remember her day being acknowledged by me or anyone else, though I'm sure my siblings showered her with cards. Now I had yet another reason to be angry with Michael.

# My Old Church

Well, the week waned, and it was soon Sunday again. The children and I went to my old church with Mom. It was a blessing to see my old church family, and they were just as happy to see us. It felt good to be home. I felt safe and loved. They didn't have a clue of what was going on in my life, but by my testimony, they knew I was in trouble and would be home for a while. Through their excitement, I heard the Holy Spirit speak to my spirit that I wouldn't be there long.

In no time, it was Monday morning and I had to make that dark, hour-long drive to Fort Wayne to work. It was dark because, at that time, we were on different time zones: Fort Wayne was an hour behind Ohio. I drove to work in the dark, and by the time I got off work and headed back to Lima, it was evening and dark again. There were times I'd fall asleep while driving and run off the road. It was getting tough to make that drive every day, Monday through Friday. My children only saw me on the weekends; they'd be asleep when I left, and asleep when I returned. It was wearing Mom out to have two little ones to care for. Though she had retired by this time, she wasn't used to having two little ones running around the house.

One day, my mother said, "You need to get yourself together. These children are miserable." My daughter had apparently told Mom, "Grandma, we hate being at your house." I'm sure that hurt

Mom's feelings, but she understood what her little granddaughter meant. She was trying to say that she wanted to be in her own house, sleeping her own bed, and eating the food and snacks she and her brother were accustomed to. They were tired of greens and cornbread, neckbones, liver and onions, fish with rice and all the other down-home foods Mom would cook. They wanted some ravioli, spaghetti, hot dogs, fried chicken, mashed potatoes, and fruit snacks. I heard Mom and I heard my daughter, but I didn't know when I'd be going back. Bottom line: we were homeless.

There were times, when I went to work, that Michael would be waiting for me outside my office building. He looked so bad, I hardly recognized him. His beard was overgrown, and he was thin as a rail. He looked like a bum. What a drastic difference from the man I met and married, who was very particular about his hair and clothes, and always smelled good because he wore the best cologne. I was embarrassed and didn't want him to say anything to me. I hurried into the building to get away from him as I mumbled under my breath, "Stay away from my job, I don't want to see you" He wanted to know how the children were doing, but I never responded. I didn't want to hear his voice. There was nothing more he could say to me. I was *done!* Hate raged in my heart. It was an awful emotion, and I didn't want to die with my heart in that condition for I knew I'd be lost forever. I didn't want to hate, but I didn't know how not to hate. What a mess!

# I Heard, but Now I See

I was in the rut and rat race, driving back and forth to keep my job. The weekends were a bittersweet relief. I was happy to not be on the highway and able to spend some time with my children, whom I'd missed so much. I felt so bad for them. They didn't know what to think. I'd never wanted to raise my children in such chaos and instability, from pillar to post, here and there and nowhere, no place to call home. It depressed me. I kept praying for direction and a breakthrough.

One Sunday in December, while sitting in the worship service, I opened my Bible to nowhere in particular, and landed on Job 42:5. It read:

> I have heard of thee by the hearing of the ear: but now
> mine eye seeth thee.

Here came the tears; I started bawling like a baby. I knew the Holy Spirit was telling me my time in Lima was up. The book of Job is an awesome testimony of the power of God in times of despair and chaos. Job lost all ten of his children on the same day. He went bankrupt in one day when all his livestock were killed. His body was afflicted with boils from the crown of his head to the soles of his feet. But through his suffering and his willingness to forgive his foolish wife (who told him to curse God and die), and his accusatory friends who said he must have sinned to deserve such painful suffering, Job endured. He trusted the Lord and remained faithful. In this, the final chapter of the book, he chose to forgive his friends, and the Lord gave him double the wealth he had lost, blessing him with ten more children. Job concluded that he'd heard about the power of God from others, but now, he was able to *see* God's power for himself.

Trouble has a way of opening our eyes, allowing us to see God and ourselves in a way that we'd never seen before. Trouble brings out the truth. We have to face our truth, and deal with it. Blinking back the tears, I rose up to let my church family know that I was heading back to Fort Wayne. I didn't have a date, but I knew my time was up, and I must face the music and go back.

"What are you going to do?" Mom asked. I told her I didn't know, but I was sure the Lord was speaking to me through Job 42:5. She assured me that I could stay with her as long as I needed. I knew I could, but I wanted to obey the Holy Spirit. I knew in my spirit that blessings won't follow you unless you're in the will of God. I couldn't receive my breakthrough if my breakthrough were in Fort Wayne, and I remained in Lima. I had to be in the place of my breakthrough.

# Foreclosure

Shortly after that Sunday, maybe early the next week, while working in my office, I was surprised with a phone call from the mortgage company. They called to let me know the home was in foreclosure. I listened but didn't care because my husband was in the home and the mortgage was so far behind, there was no way I'd be able to save the house on my salary.

As she shared the numbers and read all the other legalities, I preoccupied myself with the work on my desk and wasn't paying much attention at all until she said, "We are willing to work with you, if you want to save your home." Again, there went the tears. I couldn't believe what I was hearing. I asked if she would repeat herself. I asked what I needed to do to save the house. I informed her that I had no extra money to put down to get it out of foreclosure. She worked a plan I couldn't refuse: no down payment, pay the same monthly payment and $50 each month towards the arrears until it was caught up. You already know—more tears! I was in my office, trying not to draw attention to myself because no one would understand. In fact, no one except my boss knew what was going on. The woman from the mortgage company informed me that they had already evicted my husband, and the house was empty. She warned me that it was in pretty bad shape, with no utilities except water, and it was dirty and in disarray. I asked how soon I could come back, and she said any time. I just had to let her know when, and she'd have the keys ready for me.

# No Place like Home

I could hardly wait to get back to Mom's and tell her the news. My heart was racing as I drove back to Lima. I was happy and scared—happy to be able to get my children in a more stable environment, back to their beds and the comfort of their own home. I was scared because I didn't know where I would get the money to get the gas and lights back on. It was winter and a week before Christmas.

On Sunday, December 18, 1988, I packed up my car and drove westward across Highway 30, bawling the entire way. I was so grateful to mom and Mr. Chester for allowing us to intrude on their privacy and peace. It was on a Sunday, Mom's birthday when I arrived in Lima and a Sunday, on my friend's birthday, when I returned to Fort Wayne.

Just before we left to reclaim our home, something happened that let me know that I was going to see the power of God working on our behalf. My uncle Quince, Mom's older brother, was apparently feeling the spirit of Christmas—he didn't normally and hadn't done since I'd graduated from high school. He sent me three crisp one-hundred-dollar bills with a short note that said, "Get the kids something for Christmas—Quince." I hadn't heard from him since my graduation, over six years before. He didn't have a clue what I was going through. But God is a spirit, and when He works in the earth, He uses *people*. He will use other people to give to you, or to help you get what you need to fulfill your purpose and destiny; that time, he used my uncle Quince. I felt like Job. *Now* my eyes were seeing what Job saw: the power of *the God of restoration*!

Have you guessed, by now, the gift the children got for Christmas? Yep, you guessed right: heat and lights. I was able to use that money to get my utilities turned back on. I had heard others sharing the miraculous things that had happened in their lives, but now *my* eyes were able to see the power of God, working miracles in *my* life. Blessed be God! I was so grateful for my uncle Quince.

I had the keys, the utilities were on, and though the house was yet in disarray, it felt good to be home. The children ran up and down the stairs, screaming and laughing. They were happy to be home. I agreed with them: *there's no place like home.*

# I Don't Want To

Christmas came and went, and the new year was just around the corner. I waited in anticipation, glad to see 1988 pass away, never to return. It took a while, but eventually, I had a smile back on my face and I was feeling hopeful. I was so happy to be able to drive just five minutes up the street to work, versus over an hour there and an hour back, every day and night. That alone was a huge blessing. Thank you, Jesus!

Mom called daily to check on us. After a few weeks, when she saw that we were doing great, she started calling just once a week. She was relieved to know we were doing okay and had a warm place to stay and food to eat. Occasionally, she would send money in a card with a note to say, "It's not much, but it's a little something to keep the 'haints' off of you." I had no clue what haints were, but I sensed they weren't good if she was trying to keep them away from me. She used to say that all the time when I was a young girl. I later found out that the haints were evil spirits that originated in the customs and beliefs of the Gullah Geechee people, descendants of African slaves who lived in the Carolinas, Georgia, and northern Florida. Did Mom know this? I don't know. She never explained what haints were, that I remember. Perhaps her mother passed it down to her. Whatever the case, she would send cash money in the mail to help out.

It didn't take my husband long to find out that I had moved back into the house, but he didn't bother us. After several weeks with no word, he finally called. He said he'd been giving a lot of deep thought about the destruction he had caused, how his life had derailed, and his disappointment over how things had gone and were going for him. By this time, he was out of the cold and living with a friend. At least that's what he said. I'd never known him to have any friends. No one ever came to the house or called him, that I'd ever seen or heard. He'd occasionally drop some names of friends from high school or "back in the day," as he'd say, but they weren't currently in his life, and I'd never met any of them. He was definitely a loner. He loved being by himself and didn't go anywhere but work and home. He never talked to anyone besides me and the children and a few people at the church when he was attending. Now that I think about it, that lifestyle created the perfect storm for him to become a drug addict.

He reviewed the happenings of the past three years, apologized, and asked me to forgive him and to give him another chance. He said he loved his family, and only ever wanted to be a family man who loved and took care of us. He said he was ashamed of himself and all the chaos he'd caused. He did most of the talking; I just listened. In fact, I didn't pay much attention because we'd been down this lane before, and I didn't trust anything he was saying. He talked on and on, at times repeating himself. He said he realized that he couldn't stop his addiction without the help of the Lord. He said he was tired of fighting and ending up back where he didn't want to be. He had maximized his visits to the treatment centers; they wouldn't allow him to come anymore. They'd say, "You know the twelve steps, you just need to work through the steps." We had Bible study on Tuesday nights, and he asked if I'd pick him up. *I didn't want to*—but I agreed. I could never have peace, refusing a ride to anyone who wanted to go to the house of the Lord.

That Tuesday, I picked him up and to my surprise, during Bible study, he asked the church to forgive him, and asked if he could be restored back in right fellowship with the church, and as a member of the Body of Christ. The pastor and the members who were there clapped their hands in praise that the prodigal son was returning home. I didn't know whether to join in the clapping or start crying in fear. I must have sat in a daze because I don't remember doing either.

When I took him back to his friend's apartment, we sat in the car and talked for a few minutes. As he wrapped up the conversation, he commented that he'd felt a heavy burden lift after asking the church and the Lord to forgive him, and how hopeful he felt about the changes of this new year, and on and on, until he asked, "Can I come back home?"

My heart was racing, and my blood was heating up. *"Come home?* You mean *right now?"* I asked.

He said, "Yes, I've asked the Lord and the church to forgive me. I'm a changed man. I'm done with drugs and the streets. I love my family, and I want to come home."

I didn't want to let him, but the Holy Spirit wouldn't let me fix my mouth to say no, so, against my will, I said, "Okay." He hurried out of the car and flew into the apartment. He got his little bag of belongings, and back to the house we drove. I drove slowly, thinking, *what have I done? Mom and my family are going to ridicule me for letting him come back.* My mind was racing a thousand miles a minute. I didn't want to reach home, but we finally got there, and went to bed.

That night, fear had a strong hold of me. I slept with my purse, so Michael wouldn't steal my bank card or check book. I couldn't sleep; he couldn't sleep. We tossed and turned, flipped, and flopped. Finally, we started talking. I was in tears and so was he; together we sobbed uncontrollably. To be honest, I felt tricked. I thought it was all a set-up to get back in the house—his call out of the blue, his wanting to go to a Bible study, his asking the Lord and church to forgive him. Yes, *I've been set up for a setback*, I thought to myself.

When I calmed down enough to talk without crying, I told Michael that there was only one way this marriage could work.

He had to get a job and get one quick. He needed to sign his uncashed checks over to me, and the bank account must remain in my name—the same for the utilities. If he left the house, he had to call me when he arrived at his destination. I'd only give him $10 in pocket money, and he had to bring a receipt to confirm how he'd spent it. Without thought or hesitation, he agreed, just like that. I didn't know what to think. He didn't have any decent clothing, so I went to Kmart and bought him some penny loafers, a pair of pants, a shirt, and a winter coat. I took all the tags and hid all the receipts, for fear that he'd try to take the items back for cash as he'd done in the past.

# The God of Restoration

Michael kept his promises. He soon found work and gave me his check. He started faithfully attending worship, Bible study, and Sunday school. When he attended a young men's fellowship at someone's home, he called me to let me know when he had arrived. He accepted the $10 allowance that I'd give him each week. He walked the tightrope with no complaints. Praise Jesus! I was still a skeptic, though, and still slept with my purse. As January ended, as February and March came and went, even though life was getting better and there was less tension between us, I didn't let my guard down, and I never let my purse out of my sight.

I can't remember how long it was before we were actually intimate, but the first time he touched me, I cried. It didn't feel right. I didn't want to, but I gave in because he'd been keeping his promise, trying to regain my trust, and I didn't want to discourage him and send him backwards. God forbid! It was stressful, but we made it through.

April and May came and went, and still he kept his promise. There were no slip-ups that I was aware of. The children were so happy to have their dad back home. They were happy to be back to their daily routine. We were laughing again, and the tension in our family grew lighter and lighter. The children were too young to express themselves about all of the changes we experienced. They were happy to be back in their own home and their own beds and have their dad back. My husband noticed that our son followed him around the house. We concluded that he may have been afraid of his dad leaving us again. With each passing day, things began to feel *normal* again. Before I knew it, it was our wedding anniversary month: December. Things were on the up and up for us, and I was thankful to the Lord.

The new year, 1990, was right around the corner, and it seemed we were back on track, with drugs and alcohol behind us. One Sunday, it may have been sometime in mid-to-late 1989, we had a guest speaker during morning worship: Elder Powell from Grand Rapids, Michigan. I don't recall the message he preached, but it must have been an anointed word, because the congregation was up on their feet, clapping and giving God praise. After the sermon, before Elder Powell took his seat, he called my husband to the front and said the Lord wanted him to pray for Michael. When he finished his prayer, Elder Powell told Michael that the Lord was calling him to a ministry of restoration, and that God was going to use him to bless others. My husband sat down and didn't give it much thought. Those words were tucked away in his heart and never recalled again until about nine years later. I don't recall feeling one way or the other about the word through Elder Powell.

Michael continued to do well and remained faithful to his promises. One day, he finally looked at me and said, "Nita, it's been two years now. Haven't I proven myself? Can I get my name back on the checking account, the light bill, the gas bill or *something,* anything!"

We both laughed and said, "Wow, that time rolled by quickly!" Two years of clean time. God did it, just like that! I loosened the reins a little and added his name to the checking account. He no longer had to sign over his hardcopy check to me; he progressed to automatic deposit, and although I might have worried, just a little bit, everything was fine.

I don't know the day, nor the hour, but I can honestly say that the Lord placed a love in my heart for Michael that was greater than what I felt for him when we first met and married. He took away all the hatred and resentment between us and replaced it with true love—love that only the Lord can give. One day, while in prayer with thanksgiving to God for restoring our marriage, I heard that still, small voice whisper in my spirit and say, "I told you, I was going to do a new thing." Tears welled up in my eyes as I remembered back to 1986, when He'd given that message to me. It had been a long, hard road to that new thing. The Holy Spirit said He had to tear down the old before the newness of life could come. He also said, "It wasn't about the drugs and alcohol. It was about what I needed to do *in you;* there was hatred and resentment in your heart that needed to be rooted out." What the Lord was really doing was working a new thing in *me!* Many times, we say "I love you" without much thought, but do we realize what we are saying? Do we *really, truly* love unconditionally, without partiality, without keeping track of wrongs, with patience, forever? He restored my love, and my life!

Often, we point fingers and blame others for the chaos in our lives. I dare say that when you're experiencing troubles in your life, you need to take a deeper look, examine yourself, and ask the Lord to show you who you really are. Ask Him to work *out* of you everything that is not pure and holy, and work *in* you the will to do the right thing, according to His divine plan. There was ugliness hiding deep within my heart, and it took the right test to bring it to the surface. It was real and could not be denied.

Life was good and getting better with each passing day, but the Lord still had plans for me!

# The Dream

In January 1992, I heard the Lord speak during my quiet time in prayer. He said it was going to be a "year of opening doors!" *What could that mean?* I thought to myself.

> "I know thy works: behold, I have set before thee an open door, and no man can shut it: for thou hast a little strength, and hast kept my word, and hast not denied my name." (Revelations 3:8)

I didn't have a clue, but I'd seen the power of God move in the past, and I trusted that He'd do it again.

In February, I got my first inkling of what the Lord had in store. I don't recall the date, but I had a very disturbing dream. I don't claim to be a dreamer and wasn't known to have very many dreams. This was one that disturbed me. All I saw was the profile of a man. Some say we don't dream in color, but I saw he was a good-looking gentleman, wearing a nice olive-colored suit, bearded, with a fair amount of hair on his head. It wasn't a big afro, nor was it a buzz cut. He was a stranger; I knew I'd never seen him before. It was several weeks before I shared the dream with my husband, because I was afraid that he'd think I was lusting after another man. He had no idea what it meant, either. I tried to forget the dream, but it wouldn't go away.

One day, I had lunch with Sister Patti. We were talking about the same things we always talked about, when she began to share some concerns that reminded me of my dream. She loved the Lord and could, many times, give interpretation to others' dreams, so I began to share mine with her. As I described the man in my dream, she pulled out a business card and asked, "Is this the man?"

I began to break out in chills, then a sweat. I was stricken with disbelief; I didn't know whether to stand up or sit down, laugh or cry. The man in my dream was a real person, and *his picture was on that business card!* I took a closer look at the card and dropped it in disbelief. His city and state address read Mt. Vernon, New York—*the exact same city my mother had told me my father was from.* My friend was aware of my desire to find my father, but it was obvious that the man on the card was too young to be my father and the name didn't match my father's name.

We had other things to discuss, and we did, but I was haunted by what had just happened. I think I asked for the card or his phone number. I was so flustered at the time that I don't recall, but I told my husband about it and he encouraged me to call the man.

# The First Call

It took a while, but that February, I got up enough nerve to call the man I'd seen in the dream. I shared my story, told him how I got his number, and that I thought he could help me find my father. By this time, I was twenty-eight years old. He said, "Well, I'm a traveling evangelist and I'm not in New York much, but I'll do what I can to help you." I was satisfied with that response, thanked him for his time and consideration, calmly hung up the phone…and then started screaming all the way to the moon and back. I called to mind the word that the Lord had given me the month before about opening doors. I could hardly contain my excitement and called my mother to tell her about the dream and the call. Remember, she'd prayed to the Lord to let her live until I found my dad. It seemed to us that God had heard both of our prayers. I felt so hopeful!

# The Second Call

Spring came and went, then June, then July…and I hadn't heard anything from the evangelist. It was August, and still no response. I was becoming discouraged. I knew it didn't make sense. After all, I had been waiting twenty-eight years. What was another six months? But when you finally have hope that you'll receive an answer to prayer you'd never expected, every moment until that answer comes seems to last *so* long.

On Friday, August 7, 1992, I was at work when my office phone rang. I was a few offices away from mine, working with a colleague, so it was a miracle that I even heard it, let alone that I made it back to my desk before it stopped. It was the evangelist, calling to let me know he'd found the man I was looking for. It was a shame to be at work during that call because I was just *bursting* with excitement. I wanted to *scream* for pure joy!

My heart was racing a thousand miles a minute as I wrote down the information he'd discovered. He told me where my father worshipped, his birthday, his age, and, I believe, his address. He then told me where my father worked and said that he had gone to his job to pay him a visit. He said he'd given my dad my phone number and then said, "The ball is in his court. I pray he calls." When we hung up, I ran back to the office where I was working with a co-worker and told a skinny version of my story. Suddenly, big tears began to drop to her desk. I was taken aback and asked why she was crying. She shared what I was starting to realize was a common experience. I'd heard it from almost every sixth or seventh person I'd shared my story with. She told me that the man she lived with wasn't her father; the irony in her story was that she knew, but her father didn't.

I was so excited about finding my father that I even wrote to Ms. Winfrey and shared my story, hoping to be invited to her show. She did send an acknowledgement postcard, but I never received an invitation to appear on her show. I thought it was a good enough story for television, but the Lord didn't suffer it to be so. I was a little disappointed, but at the same time, I didn't really care. I just wanted the whole world to know that I was lost, but now I'd been found.

# The Third Call

Once I'd heard from the evangelist, I was certain that I'd hear from my father right away, perhaps even that very day. Well, two days passed, and my dad still hadn't called. I was getting discouraged. Didn't my father want to find me too?

That Sunday, August 9, 1992, the worship service at our church was exceptional. The presence of the Holy Spirit filled the sanctuary. I was overwhelmed by His presence. Out of nowhere, I began to head to the microphone to sing "I've Got a Feeling That Everything's Gonna Be Alright." No one invited me to sing, I just went as I felt the Holy Spirit leading me. I sang and sang until the saints broke out in a dance, giving God a high praise. I was weeping and crying, as I sang. I'd never done anything like that before. After everyone calmed down, the pastor dismissed us to go home.

When I got home, I finished cooking dinner, washed the dishes, and began talking to my husband about the call from the evangelist. As we talked, I began to bawl like a baby. "Everyone should know their father!" I cried.

In the past, when we talked about my desire to know who my father was, my husband would remind me that he didn't know his father, either; he had passed when Michael was three years old. I know my husband meant to be consoling, but it just made me feel worse. I still wanted to find my father and knowing that Michael would never know his sparked my fears that the same thing could happen to me. I didn't care if he was dead or alive or if he didn't want to have anything to do with me, I told myself. I just wanted to *know*. Well, it was a special blessing to know that he was alive and still in Mt. Vernon, New York, but now I knew that that was not going to be enough. I needed *more*.

While I lay on the floor crying, the phone rang. My husband answered, and held the receiver out to me, smiling. Lo and behold, it was my father! I was so overcome, I dropped the phone and continued bawling. Through my sobs, I could hear Michael, telling me to pick up the phone and talk—this was the call I had been waiting on for twenty-eight years. I managed to pull myself together to finish the call. His voice was deep. While I was hyped, he seemed very calm. I remember his first words: "Hello, this is your dad." I was crying so loud, I couldn't tell if he cried or not. He later admitted that he was very nervous about all the happenings and making the first call. I thought to myself that I couldn't tell. We didn't have much to say. It was very awkward, to say the least. Believe me, when we hung up, I was *way* past cloud nine. I'm sure I reached Cloud 100! I immediately called Mom to share the great news. Mom was overjoyed! She had prayed to live until I found him. What a relief she felt! She endured many years of emotional stress, wanting to tell me the truth while being torn by the promise she made to Deddy that she would never tell me the truth as long as he lived.

Periodically, my father and I would talk on the phone. We also exchanged addresses and wrote each other in between calls. He sent me photos and I sent him photos. It was truly a dream come true! Who could orchestrate such things? *The God of restoration*! He can, and He did!

# The Trip

It was so natural to call him Dad. He apologized for not being there as I grew up, but I wasn't bothered by that at all. I told him that there was nothing we could do about the past; the best thing to do was to move forward and enjoy the time that we had left.

I wanted to see him in person. Dad wanted to meet us, too. Mom wanted to go along and of course, my husband was going with me. That was three airplane tickets. I was worried about the expense of the trip until I heard the Lord remind me that He was going to help me find my dad, and it wasn't going to cost me a dime. Well, for sure, God kept his promise and helped me find him without paying a private investigator, but now I wanted to see him face to face. Surely that hadn't been included.

I worked in Human Resources and knew that my company had a jet that the employees could book as long as we were flying per the corporation's schedule. In other words, we couldn't customize our own trip, but we could ride along if the jet was already traveling somewhere. I checked the schedule for flights to New York and found an upcoming one in early November, going to White Plains. I called Dad to see how far that was from Mt. Vernon and he said it was "up the road." I guessed that meant it wasn't far, and wouldn't you know, it was 13.9 miles north of Mt. Vernon. Only a Mighty

God could operate with such precision to orchestrate these events. I booked three seats, and we were on our way. Thankfully, the schedule allowed us to spend two whole days and return on day three.

Here's the beauty bonus: we flew on a plush Lear jet as the only passengers aboard, and we didn't have to purchase tickets. The price was added to my gross income and taxed through payroll.

Dad was super late picking us up from the airport. I started to get nervous, and the evil one planted seeds of doubt in my mind that he wasn't going to show up. He finally got there, almost two hours late, pulling up in a cab. His timing chain had broken while he was on the highway. Had it not been for the rain, he may have been able to fix it since he was a master mechanic, but he ended up leaving the car on the side of the road and catching a cab. The cab driver was so intrigued by our story, he waited for Dad to greet us and drove us back to Dad's house. When we got to Dad's apartment, the cab driver refused payment. He told us to have a happy life. Dad was offended that we were going to book a hotel and we ended up staying at his place. God did it! I don't think we spent $10 between the three of us.

Mom accidently left her inhaler either on the jet or at my house, and even though it was a rainy day, and we had dinner in a smoky restaurant, she never once wheezed or needed her inhaler. Praise Jesus!

In New York, I met aunts, uncles, and other family for the first time. I learned that I had eight or nine other siblings, and I would eventually meet all of them, with the exception of one brother. We were able to meet the evangelist who'd helped me find my father, and his friend. We had dinner with the evangelist and learned that his apartment was in the same neighborhood as my dad's—literally up the street and around the corner. You could walk to either place in six minutes or less. Who orchestrates these precise events? *The God of restoration!* There is absolutely *nothing* God cannot restore and *no* thing He cannot redeem. I dare you to trust Him and see—won't

He do it! If he did it for me, He can do it (whatever your "it" may be) for you.

The evangelist actually ended up spending Thanksgiving with us. He was in Fort Wayne, running a revival for a church that was a block south of my house. I could walk there in less than five minutes. He said he had run several revivals for them before I'd contacted him to help me find my father. He was well-acquainted with that assembly; he knew the people and the people knew him. Again, who could orchestrate such precise events? *The God of restoration!* He can do anything!

# The Breakdown

By the winter of 1996, I had been promoted several times on my job. I had gone from Supervisor of Payroll to Field Consultant (where I flew all over the country to our regional offices to conduct human resources-related training), then to Account Manager, where I managed million-dollar retirement accounts for over 100 companies. I worked long hours—ten to twelve-hour days—and most nights. I had also been promoted to leadership responsibilities in the ministry of our church that required me to travel regionally and sometimes nationally. I was all over the place, doing this and that, still responsible for the administration of my local church. I had active children who were approaching adolescence. I was active in their lives, too, with sporting events, band, choir, school volunteering, PTA meetings, and you name it. I didn't want them to grow up and say that no one had been there to support them. I didn't want them to be the children who didn't have a ride home because their parents weren't there. Additionally, I was a Big Sister for Big Brothers-Big Sisters; I was a volunteer for Junior Achievement and spent one day for six successive weeks in various classrooms teaching students the "Economics of Staying in School." I was the Sunday school teacher, the butler, baker, and candlestick maker. Whew! How did I ever keep up? Only by the grace of God! I didn't look at the big picture; I couldn't. I only focused on the task at hand.

One morning, before work, my husband and I had a big blow up about all of the above. He was frustrated because I had very little time for him. My remedy was for him to get up and join me. Instead of staying home all the time with no one but the TV, refusing to participate in all of our activities, I suggested he travel with me, or that we volunteer as a team. There was nothing I did that he couldn't do or help do, nor a place that I traveled where he couldn't join me. He didn't want to do anything except go to work, go to church, and then go back home. We had very different interests. I'm an artsy person. I loved music and grew up in the school band, playing the clarinet, oboe, and saxophone. I tried my hand at piano and organ but didn't go very far, but I was always ready to try something new. My husband was not as adventurous, or as outgoing. He preferred a quieter life.

By the time I got to work, I was beat down, stressed out, and frustrated. Tears began to well up in my eyes. I had a migraine headache and was feeling sick. I was so overwhelmed, I felt like I was going to lose my mind. I was, literally, a hot mess. I couldn't focus on my work. I didn't want to go back home. I called one of my spiritual mothers and told her what had happened and how I was feeling. She reserved a cab to come get me and I stayed with her for about three or four days.

No one knew where I was. After twenty-four hours, my husband called the police and reported me missing. The police were looking for me. My co-workers spent hours looking for me. They looked throughout the building, checking the bathrooms, the closets, the stairwells. They reviewed the surveillance camera and saw what time I entered the building and the time I left, but nothing else. People met at my house, bringing food, having prayer vigils and the whole nine. It was unbelievable.

While they were gathered at my house, I was with my spiritual mother, fighting for my sanity. I lay balled in a fetal position, moaning like an animal, praying to the Lord to help me keep my mind. It was horrific. I used to wonder how people wound up walking to nowhere, talking to themselves, and staring at nothing. Well, I don't wonder anymore; the way I felt, I was about to be one of them. I was being attacked from all angles. My spiritual mother didn't know what she could do besides pray. I did manage to ask her to call my mother to let her know I was safe, but I didn't want anyone else to know where I was. I didn't even think about my children and how they must be feeling, wondering if their mother was dead or alive.

At that point, I didn't care about anything. I just wanted to die. I wanted to kill myself, but I remembered that the scriptures taught me, "Thou shalt not kill." I didn't want to risk being eternally lost. I spent those days in fog between here and somewhere. I'm glad I never actually found out what that "somewhere" was.

I had always been a person who preferred having things organized and in their respective places; when they weren't, it was very stressful for me. I don't know what changed, but when I rose up from that stupor, I had made a 180-degree turn. I went from one end of the spectrum to the other. I was always on my husband and the children about picking up their belongings and returning them to the proper place. "Pick up your shoes, put your book bag up, pick up that paper, wash the dishes, clean your room," and on and on. Nobody seemed to care about all those things but me. After my emotional breakdown, however, I didn't care about anything. For several weeks, I ignored all of the messes, just like the rest of my family. I stepped over things that were left in the floor, just like they were doing. I didn't have the wherewithal to bother with it anymore.

After about three weeks of total chaos and confusion, my husband blew up. He stopped everything and ordered the children to help him clean up all the messes. I didn't budge or say a word. I had a new slogan: "When I die, I'm going to die a happy woman!" I wasn't going to let anything upset me to *that* point ever again. I was about to lose my mind, but *the God of restoration* rescued me! My heart is compassionate towards those who suffer mental illness. It's real.

# The Ministry of Restoration

In 1989, after being delivered and reclaimed from a backslidden state of crack and alcohol addiction, my husband received a prophetic word from Elder James that God was calling him to a ministry of restoration. Early in 1990, a second prophecy was received through my friend, Sister Penny, that we would jointly shepherd this ministry. We didn't know exactly what this ministry was going to be, however, and so we waited on the Lord to reveal more of His plan for us.

In 1998, I started to feel a sense of restlessness and oppression in my spirit. I found myself wanting to cry, but the tears wouldn't come. When I left my family's home in Lima to attend college in Fort Wayne, I had no intention of making it my final destination. I'd planned to go at least as far as Colorado, but then, of course, I ended up getting married instead. I still wanted to see more of the world, however, and in the early years of our marriage, I even suggested to Michael that he join the military, just so we could leave town for somewhere more exciting. But he wasn't interested in moving then, and he certainly wasn't hearing it now.

I was at work one afternoon during this time when I heard the tail end of a radio broadcast message from The Leadership Series. The teacher said, "Stick with your leader; God may not be glorified, but He's at work." Immediately, tears welled up in my eyes and I wept at my desk. I knew the Lord was telling me I wasn't going anywhere soon. Right then and there, I surrendered my will and submitted to the will of the Lord. I resolved to be content with the place He had put me and went on my way.

Later that year, we received further affirmation of our calling when God used our assistant pastor, Elder Benson, who had no foreknowledge of what we had been told before. In his message, he confirmed that we should obey God's plan for us, adding that, when we were called, we should obey God and not worry about what people would say. On November 13, 1998, Bishop Dupree, who had been our pastor since I arrived in Fort Wayne, passed away, and the church was up for new leadership. The next April, during our Women's Day meeting, the Holy Ghost confirmed our pastoral calling through our speaker, Co-Pastor Jefferson. It was then that Michael and I knew the time had come for our ministry to begin.

By this time, Pastor Bust had been installed as the church's new pastor. We met with him shortly after his installation to let him know we'd be leaving by the end of the year to follow our calling. I don't remember if he ever gave us his blessing, but we had to do what we felt the Lord was leading us to do. It was a bittersweet departure, because my husband had been born and raised in that church, and I had been there for eighteen years. But I was reminded of that radio sermon from two years before: "Stick with your leader; God may not be glorified, but He's at work." Now we saw the working of the Lord with our own eyes.

On January 2, 2000, we held our first worship service at a local YMCA, with twelve members, including my husband, our two children, and me. It felt different but liberating. We had no formal training, but we were teachable and wanted to please God. By December of that year, God blessed us to move into another building on the north side of town. We were blessed in that place until December 2003, when we were asked to move because the property was being sold. The Lord was faithful and blessed us through another divine connection with Dad Hayden. He was instrumental in recommending that we share worship facilities with his local Methodist church, where he faithfully served. We shared that space until we were ready to purchase our own building. It was a wonderful experience.

God shut the mouths of the naysayers who said our ministry was too young, and that no bank would loan us any money. After months of searching and praying, the Lord blessed us to close on our new location on Thursday, June 23, 2005. After fifteen years, by God's grace, we were able to pay off the building's mortgage during the summer of 2020. Who could orchestrate such precise events and prophesies? *The God of restoration!*

# He Passed Away

Dad and I enjoyed sweet fellowship for ten wonderful years. He would often share about what a bad person he was before he found the Lord. I would respond that we were all bad until we found the Lord. Who can cast the first stone? Everybody's got a skeleton or two in their closet that they are ashamed to share. I didn't want to focus on the past. I loved him, and he loved me, and that was all that mattered.

Grown as I was, I found he still had some fatherly wisdom for me. One thing I often mention is his wise teaching that we should never talk about or make fun of others because it's a bad reflection on God, as if He didn't know what He was doing to give them dark skin, a wide nose, fat lips, and a head full of grey hair. No one got a chance to choose his or her profile; it came from the Creator. Love them anyway and thank God because what you laugh at could be you. I was speechless when he told me that; I'd never looked at it that way before, and now I make sure to share that advice with others whenever I can.

In the late summer of 2001, I experienced an unrest in my spirit. My dad was on my mind, and I shared with my husband that I felt led to make a trip to visit with him. He encouraged me to follow my heart. I cleared my work calendar and got things in order to be gone for a week. I confirmed Dad's location during the week of September 10, and he told me he'd be in the Carolinas to see his doctor. I told him to stay there until my visit was over because I was headed that way.

I boarded a plane on Monday, September 10, 2001, and headed to the Carolinas. I rented a car and drove about seventy-five miles to Lynn's, where Dad was staying while in the Carolinas. Lynn was like a daughter to my dad. It was a nice ride. I was so happy to see Dad, and he was happy to see me. We sat up until the wee hours of the morning, laughing and talking.

I slept in until about 10:00 or 11:00 the next morning. When I got up, I was surprised to find Dad sitting on the floor, with his eyes glued to the TV. I asked him what was going on and he said, "Someone just flew a plane into the twin towers." Oh my, what a tragedy! We were all glued to the TV for hours and hours, trying to make sense of this act of terrorism. They closed all airports and called for a state of emergency for the entire country. Somebody was out to get us.

My husband and the children were upset and called, suggesting that they rent a car to drive down to get me, since the airports were closed. I didn't want to leave; I had just gotten there, and I wanted to spend time with Dad. My husband relented and agreed to ride the week out to see what would happen. I know we all held our breath for a few days after the attacks, but in the end, I was safe, and all was well.

One morning during my visit, I drove Dad to pick up some medicine and he began to sing a tune under his breath. I asked, "What are you singing?"

He raised his voice and started sing loudly, "This may be my last time, it may be my last time, I don't know."

I asked him to pick another song because that song made me sad. He mildly rebuked me and said, "I don't know what you're talking about, it may be *your* last time, you don't know." I agreed since none of us knows when our time is up on this earth. Thus, it behooves us to love and forgive others, to do the right thing for the right reasons, and to love God with all of our hearts. If you do these things, you'll die with no regrets. After my emotional breakdown, I was reminded how short life is, and that whatever I needed to do to fulfill my purpose, I'd better get busy.

That week with Dad passed by quickly. Before I knew it, it was time for me to return home. By that time, most airports had reopened with major restrictions, but they were eerily empty—none of the hustling and bustling you would expect—and the few travelers I saw seemed subdued and nervous. I must admit, I was also nervous. I had a nice flight back and smiled as I reminisced about the sweet time I got to spend with my father. But once I touched down in Indiana, it was back to the rat race of work and all the other things I had going on.

Fall went by quickly, and winter started doing its thing. I talked to Dad periodically, and one day, he told me he had cancer—bone cancer, I believe. He said he was in a lot of pain on a regular basis, and that he could find very little relief. I felt so helpless. As we talked, I could hear, in my spirit, the song he sang while I was visiting him, just a few months ago. Tears welled up in my eyes and began to fall on my shirt. It was all I could do to keep from breaking down while talking to him, but I didn't want him to know I was crying. He talked as long as he could, then we said a prayer and hung up.

On New Year's Day, 2002, I called to wish him a "Happy New Year," but things weren't so happy for him. He could only talk about his health, and he told me that he was tired and ready to give up. When we hung up, I sobbed like a child because I knew that this truly was his—our—last time. Again, deep within my soul, I could hear him singing, "This may be my last time, it may be my last time, I don't know." I bawled even more. My tears weren't so much of sadness as they were of gratitude. I was so thankful that the Lord had allowed us ten precious years together. I'll treasure those memories of my father as long as I live.

The next phone call I received from New York came on January 4, 2002, from my Aunt Ola, who informed me that Dad had passed away. I was speechless, but strangely, I didn't cry. I couldn't; I had cried all the tears I had left for him. All I could do was sit in silence and give God praise for loving me so much that he honored my mom's prayer to allow me to find my father before she passed away. Mom was a jewel. She went on to live twenty-seven more years after me finding my father. Who could orchestrate such precise events? *The God of restoration!* For sure, He's alive and working on our behalf.

# The Queen Passes Away

Well, as you can see, my life has never been a quiet one. There's always been something going on—good, bad, and ugly—but God has assured me that nothing is wasted with Him. All things are working together for my good, because I love Him.

Now we fast forward, from 2002 to 2020. Wow, isn't that interesting? Same numbers, different order: 2002 and 2020.

I want you to walk with me through these miraculous ten months of 2020. Today, is Friday, October 16, 2020. It's 10:32 p.m. and I've been locked away in the Wyndham Hotel for three days, writing this book almost non-stop, with mini- breaks in between. My hands are tired, and my legs are aching from sitting so long My stopwatch says 13:21:15— yes, I've been writing today for thirteen-plus hours, writing the book that I dreamed I'd write, over twenty-five years ago. Who has a dream that long ago about writing a book, not knowing what it would be about, just seeing the title, *The God of Restoration*? And who goes on to actually write that book? Me, Anita Marie!

I must not leave tomorrow without being totally finished. Finished means the writing's complete, the publishing forms are filled out, and the whole thing is emailed to my publisher—who by the way, has been paid in full and waiting on my manuscript since May 2019. Writing a book sounds easy, like anyone could do it—until that writer is *you*.

Shortly after I signed with my publisher, the very next month in fact, I called a family meeting with my siblings to discuss how we would care for Mom. She was ninety-three and still living independently, but with old and new health concerns. I tried to get her to come to Indiana and live with me, for a while at least, even if she didn't want to stay forever. She preferred to stay in Lima. It was upsetting to me, but I had to release it to the Lord. It was way too heavy for me to bear.

As a result of our meeting, I agreed to drive an hour to Mom's on Mondays and Fridays every week to help her with chores, cooking, and to spend quality time with her. This would give my oldest sister a break. She had been Mom's main contact and help for over fifteen years. She had gone well over and above the call of duty in caring for Mom and done a great job of it. Fortunately, by this time, the Lord had released me from my job; I retired after 32 years. Whew, what a blessing! That's another book and I won't go into those details, but it was nothing short of a miracle. Occasionally I ran into schedule conflicts, but for the most part, I was with Mom every Monday and Friday. My husband was very supportive and encouraged me to see about Mom, for which I'll be forever grateful. It meant so much.

On Friday, October 25, 2019, Mom had a doctor's appointment and was ordered to go from the office straight to the emergency room. There, she had an ultrasound on her leg to determine if she had a blood clot, as she had swelling that lingered and wouldn't seem to let up. Long story short, she was admitted to the hospital and for the next two weeks, it was a rollercoaster ride of hope and anxiety, all the way up to her homegoing on Monday, November 11, 2019. A spiritual veteran had been called up on Veteran's Day! What a legacy!

Who would ever have thought that the second oldest of six would outlive all five of her siblings? My mother suffered most of her life with asthma and had several near-death experiences. She raised six children with poor spousal assistance, rescued herself and her family from domestic violence, buried two husbands, her second oldest daughter, and two grandchildren. She lived and loved so much in her ninety-four years, and though she is gone, she will never be forgotten. I love her forever! She was my Queen Angel.

# Covid-19

As 2019 faded into 2020, we all had high hopes for the coming year. However, fate had other plans and wasted no time introducing the entire world to a wicked viral pandemic known as COVID-19.

No matter how someone tries to prepare, he or she leaves a lot undone at death, and it took me some time to finalize Mom's business. By the time I was about to see the light, Friday, March 27, 2020, popped up to smack us. I had to take my husband to the emergency room as he wasn't feeling well. The doctor suspected that he had the deadly COVID-19 virus and admitted him for testing and treatment.

Two days later, I started running a temperature and was not feeling well. It's hard to explain how it felt; I was tired and wanted to sleep most of the day. My energy was very low, I had a terrible headache, and my fever wouldn't quit. The virus was all over the news, and as I had just taken my husband to an ER filled with coughing, miserable people, I knew I might have been exposed. It was my worst fear, and it had come true. It was all downhill for me from there. I became weaker and weaker. I struggled to stay awake. I called the Board of Health for advice; they told me to quarantine for a minimum of fourteen days, because I had been in contact with my husband. We were still waiting for his test results.

*Anita M. Payton*

That Tuesday, March 31, I called my primary care physician and told her what was going on. She ordered me to go to an urgent care clinic to get a flu test. While I was there waiting, I received an urgent call from the hospital: my husband had tested positive, his breathing was compromised, and he was being transferred to the ICU. My heart dropped, and I began to pray. I called my doctor back to give her an update; she made another call back into the clinic and told them to also give me a COVID test. My husband and I were her first COVID patients.

The wait was on. While I was waiting on my results, I was being sucked in by the virus. I was so weak, I could barely hold my cell phone in my hand. I had brain fog, was dizzy, and lost my appetite. I couldn't stop coughing and coughed up so much mucus that I choked. Basically, whole nine yards—if it was listed as a COVID symptom, I believe I had it. My spiritual daughter, who was living with me at the time along with her own daughter, kept close watch over me, making sure I had everything necessary to fight the virus. At the same time, she was working from home because her office had closed as part of the quarantine and was trying to protect herself and her daughter from the virus. While she had to be nervous and tired, she checked on me regularly. I'm not sure how I would have managed without her.

While I was ill, I worked to journal my husband's own journey. I was so sick that I didn't know if I could keep up but writing everything down helped immensely. I called the hospital at least once every day, and sometimes more.

Michael's condition seemed to deteriorate by the hour. On Tuesday, March 31, they had to intubate him as his lungs were in bad shape and worsening. The virus had taken over and was wreaking havoc. He was sedated to help his body rest and heal, and so he could tolerate the tube down his throat. On Thursday, April 2, his oxygen level continued to drop, and the ventilator settings had to be increased. The high dosages of Propofol (a strong sedative used in operations) were causing his blood pressure to drop, so he had to be given new meds to stabilize his blood pressure.

Sunday, April 5—Palm Sunday—was a rough day for me. I managed to carry on the worship service that morning, but afterwards, I was so dizzy, I thought I was going to black out. I remember being in the restroom, my head swimming, and my coughing out of control. I was so sick, I truly thought this was going to be my day to go. I didn't have strength enough to raise my voice and most days barely talked above a whisper. I wanted to call out for help, but there was no way anyone could hear me. Boy, oh boy, my only help was the Lord God Almighty. I figured that if He didn't help me, I was going to die.

He did help me, and when I got myself together, I began packing a bag, in case I had to go to the hospital. I made it back to the recliner to rest. When my spiritual daughter came to check on me, I told her I was pretty sick and might have to go to the hospital. I was feeling so bad, I gave her the key to the family safe. I showed her where our life insurance policies were, and I gave her the code to my cell phone. Her eyes flew wide open, and she said, "First Lady, what's going on?" She was getting nervous. *I* was getting nervous. Sometimes, when you are that sick, you begin to doubt yourself. I called Sister Rita and Sister Beard, and they encouraged me to get up and get to the hospital. I asked my spiritual daughter to take me, and she did. There, they x-rayed me, checked my vitals, and sent me home with a Zithromax Z-pak (an antibiotic used to treat pneumonia and lung infections). I called her to come back and pick me up. I may have been there a total of two hours, at the most.

I returned home still feeling bad. The next day, Monday, April 6, I got my dreaded results and, you guessed it, I'd tested positive for the COVID-19 virus. My doctor reviewed my X-ray and called me right away to inform me that she didn't like the looks of it; she ordered me to take hydroxychloroquine (a drug used to treat malaria, lupus, and rheumatoid arthritis). It has since been disapproved as a treatment for COVID-19, but early on doctors were prescribing it. I wasn't sure how it would work for my symptoms, but I took it as prescribed. Whether or not the medicine helped, I don't know, but around April 15, I started coming back to life. My strength began to return; I was actually able to brush my teeth and shower without sitting down to take a break in between.

While I fought my own COVID battle here at the house, my husband was fighting for his life in the ICU. Prayers went up for him across the world. Family, friends, and church family were calling, bringing food, water, tea, and juice by the house and leaving it on the doorstep. Many sent money via Cash App to help wherever it was needed. I went on the Sanders Temple prayer line as often as I could, crying out to the Lord for us and others. That prayer line has been, and is, a blessing.

My husband's condition continued to deteriorate. His kidneys were in danger, with a creatinine level of 3.48 (the normal is between 0.8 and 1.4); he had to be dialyzed. His hemoglobin dropped down to six and he had to be given blood on two different occasions. I agreed with any treatment that was going to help him live, but the doctors called me twice to inform me that they had done all they could do, and he was not responding. My constant prayer was, "Lord, please don't let me have to pull the plug." I asked the doctors to give him some more time.

His condition was up and down, touch and go. It was very stressful to hear one bad report after another, but God gave him a breakthrough. On Thursday, April 23, by God's grace, they were able to take him off the ventilator. By that Saturday, they moved him to a regular room. The staff called my Michael "The Miracle Man." Many didn't think he'd make it out alive. When they told him he'd been in the hospital for thirty days—twenty-five days in ICU, and twenty-three days on the ventilator, his eyes opened wide in disbelief. I was concerned that when he was transferred to a regular room, he wouldn't get the proper attention. Sure enough, he had trouble breathing and had to be rushed back to the ICU. They thought they were going to have to put him back on the ventilator, but they didn't. Instead, they hooked him up to an Airvo, which was less invasive.

Thankfully, the staff was patient with me and my many questions. They allowed me to visit with Michael via Zoom. The first time I Zoomed in, he was in ICU on his belly, before he had to be on dialysis. He didn't even know he was in the world and said he never heard my voice. I talked to him and told him to hold on with all his might and not to let go. I sang one of his favorite songs, "Daily I Shall Worship Thee," and from then on, whether he could hear me or not, I Zoomed in whenever I could. He had awful hallucinations. He thought the police had taken his car somewhere and wouldn't tell him where it was stored. Boy, was he relieved to find out that his car was safely parked in the drive. One time, I scolded the staff because he told me that they had tied him to the bed, and he couldn't move. His nurse assured me that that was not the case, and explained they were noticing the COVID patients were suffering with hallucinations.

Michael continued to improve after his second round in ICU. On May 4—his birthday—he was released to the rehab center where he stayed for twenty-six days. My daughter and I visited with him at the window and wished him a happy birthday. He was so happy to see us! From that time on, my goal was to visit with him daily at the window. Only the staff and residents were allowed in the nursing home because of the severity of the virus. It's highly contagious and has caused the deaths of thousands. Before transferring to the nursing home for rehab, Michael was released from dialysis and the port was removed. Praise Jesus! His kidneys are totally restored. Even then, he said he wanted to give up and die because he didn't think he'd ever be able to walk again or do anything for himself, but with therapy and the Lord's help, he made it. He said therapy was hard for him and many days he didn't feel like doing it, but he was tired of being there and wanted to come home; that gave him the courage and motivation to keep going.

Well, blessed be God, he was released from the nursing home. It was Saturday, May 30 at 11:15 a.m. I had invited three news channels to come, but none showed up. I thought it was newsworthy and would encourage others who were suffering, to know that Fort Wayne had a "Miracle Man." If the news stations didn't find our story inspiring, others certainly did. I had family and friends meet me at the nursing home to surprise Michael and celebrate his release. He had no idea and was overcome with joy and tears. Thirty-eight days in the hospital, twenty-eight days in ICU, twenty-three days on the ventilator, three days on the Airvo, and twenty-six days in the nursing home for rehab. My husband *is* the Miracle Man! To make things even more special, he was released just in time for a happy Father's Day celebration at home. It was truly a wonderful time for our household.

Of course, Michael still had some work to do; his physical therapist came to our house to continue with his treatment. He had therapy twice a week, and we watched as he grew stronger and stronger. By the end of June, he had gone from not being able to walk, to the wheelchair, to a walker, to a cane and, at last, to walking on his own. By early July, his therapist released him, telling him to continue what he'd learned, and he'd get even stronger. Within a couple of weeks, he was back to driving his car and doing great. To God be the glory!

We will be forever grateful for the outpouring of prayers, love, and support we received during those trying times. Some days, we look at one another with fat tears of thanksgiving in our eyes for the miracle of life. We feel that we've both been given a second chance to fulfill our God-given purpose. We are on a mission and can't be stopped! We're COVID conquerors!

# The God of Restoration

- Restored my life back in right fellowship with Him, through the shed blood of Jesus Christ;
- Restored my marriage when it was threatened by drugs, alcohol, hatred, and resentment;
- Restored my relationship with my biological father, after twenty-eight years of separation
- Restored my mind from a mental and emotion breakdown; and
- Restored our health from COVID-19 while millions have died.

He doesn't love us any more than He loves *you*! Call on the name of Jesus and tell Him you're sorry for your sins and invite Him to be Lord of your life. Today is your day.

We're back full circle, and yet believe our undeniable testimony that He truly is the God of restoration! The best is yet to come!

> Better is the end of a thing than the beginning thereof.
> (Ecclesiastes 7:8a)

Read the following verses and make a choice to choose JESUS.

As it is written, there is none righteous, no, not one: (Romans 3:10)

For all have sinned, and come short of the glory of God; (Romans 3:23)

But God commendeth his love toward us, in that, while we were yet sinners, Christ died for us. (Romans 5:8)

Wherefore, as by one man sin entered into the world, and death by sin; and so death passed upon all men, for that all have sinned: (Romans 5:12)

For the wages of sin is death; but the gift of God is eternal life through Jesus Christ our Lord. (Romans 6:23)

But what saith it? The word is nigh thee, even in thy mouth, and in thy heart: that is, the word of faith, which we preach; That if thou shalt confess with thy mouth the Lord Jesus, and shalt believe in thine heart that God hath raised him from the dead, thou shalt be saved. For with the heart man believeth unto righteousness; and with the mouth confession is made unto salvation. For whosoever shall call upon the name of the Lord shall be saved. So then faith cometh by hearing, and hearing by the word of God. (Romans 10:8-10, 13, 17)

Then Peter said unto them, Repent, and be baptized every one of you in the name of Jesus Christ for the remission of sins, and ye shall receive the gift of the Holy Ghost. (Acts 2:38)

For by grace are ye saved through faith; and that not of yourselves: it is the gift of God: Not of works, lest any man should boast. (Ephesians 2:8-9)

All scriptures are quoted from the King James Version of the Holy Bible, unless noted otherwise.

# Bibliography

"The Gideons International," Wikipedia.com, accessed October 15, 2020, https://en.wikipedia.org/wiki/The_Gideons_International.

Printed in the United States
by Baker & Taylor Publisher Services